# FOR UNCERTAIN
# TIMES

**FORTY TRUTHS OF GOD'S CARE IN NATIONAL DISTRESS**

Jake McCandless & Rita Halter Thomas

**STAND FIRM**
*BOOKS*

# FOR UNCERTAIN TIMES

Distributed by Amazon KDP

Published by Stand Firm Books
www.standfirmministries.com

SECOND EDITION
September 11, 2022

Editor: Taryn Daley
Cover: Tyson Ranes
Section Title Art: Adobe Stock Images

A Spiritual Preparedness Resource
Spiritual Preparedness Devotional #2

ISBN: 978-1-7366746-2-8

For the hope that you *STAND FIRM*.

# TABLE OF CONTENTS

Week 3

# DISTRESS IN BABYLON

Week 4

# DISTRESS IN PERSIA

Week 5

# DISTRESS IN THE RUINS

Week 6
# DISTRESS NOW & THEN

# ACKNOWLEDGMENTS

**From Jake**

The journey of writing and publishing *For Uncertain Times* has been more than fitting for the message within it and the context of the world in which it will be released. If you've followed my writing, then you know I "write an uphill battle." My writing sessions aren't relaxing and therapeutic magical moments sipping a latte and listening to a perfectly curated pandora playlist like I dreamed of. Maybe they aren't for anyone, but I can't imagine anyone pursuing an author's life if they have to wage the war I do. Now, that probably oversells my books, but those who get in the trenches with me know this reality too well. If you want your life to fall apart, sign up to help Jake help others stand firm. If you want a front-row seat for a train wreck, join Team Jake. I wish I was exaggerating, but I'm so thankful for family and friends who are willing to hop on the train even though they know it's going off the rails. Unfortunately, I can't name all those who come aboard, but I want to thank all I can. I'll begin with my co-pilot, much better known as my wife. Amanda, you know what you've earned for the age to come. These projects have given you much opportunity to store treasures in Heaven. Thank you for your support and for holding everything together.

Andrea and Addie, I hate that these projects take me away from spending time with you. I hope that through Mom's and my heart you see Jesus is worth following and holding onto forever. And thank you for cheering Dad on!

I'm so thankful for a family that cares and is so supportive. Thank you, Mom, Dad, Kylie, Jesse, Poppa, Nana, Rodney, Melinda, and everyone I'm missing!

A big, big thank you to all who support Stand Firm and who are helping us get this message out. I'm so thankful for the congregation I pastor, Epic Church NWA. Thank you for allowing me to minister in this way.

On the writing end, I'm so honored to be represented by Cyle Young of Hartline Literary Agency. Thank you, Cyle. Rita, thank you for teaming up with me and helping my heart of helping others stand firm come to life and be readable. Taryn, thank you for getting in the trenches with us. You've been crazy patient and cleaned up our writing messes. Rita and Taryn, you've both busted your butts (Like Day #35)! We greatly missed not having Dr. Angela Ruark on board for this project, but we'll make sure she's back for future projects! Tyson, you rocked that cover! Thank you! And Eddy with the marketing—you've taken Stand Firm Books to a whole new level. Thanks for being willing to jump on this journey. I'm sure I still have something to turn into you—maybe I can get it to you tomorrow.

### From Rita

What a great honor and blessing it is to work with my friend and former pastor, Jake McCandless, on yet another exciting book project. Jake, I cannot thank you enough for allowing me the opportunity to join you in assembling *For Uncertain Times*, and our last book, *Invincible*. You are incredibly kind to give me authorship credit when you are the brains behind each book. Hopefully, I've made your messages sing and shout from the pages and earned the honor you've given me. You and Amanda shine as great ministry examples, and we are so blessed God placed you in our path. Who knew all those years ago, as we ministered to teens, that we'd find ourselves here?

I am so grateful Jake and I cohesively embrace the "mad scientist mode" that seems to produce the best work during the most critical crunch moments. We agree it is during these times God tends to show up and show out in the most incredible ways. Perhaps we begin to rely less on ourselves and more on Him in those moments—an emphasized point of every product published by Stand Firm Ministries and Stand Firm Books. We must acknowledge Him in all He has done in this book, our individual lives, and this ministry.

What can I say about the love, support, and encouragement of my husband, Jimmy? From fending for himself, serving as a sounding board, and offering grace and space during moments of intensity [A.K.A. occasional deadline irritability], thanks for carrying so much, and keeping me centered. Thanks for everything, not only on this project but all of them, and for keeping me focused in this crazy busy life. To our daughter, Marinna, for cheering me on, understanding my absence at times, and always being honest—even brutally so when necessary—to keep things real.

I echo the sentiments Jake shared of each person in the Stand Firm family–proofing, marketing, artwork, agent representation, and more—most of whom I've never met, and some only by video conference or messaging apps. You guys rock! I must say, I stand in awe watching God assemble a team of people through chance meetings, mutual acquaintances, conference encounters, and more. That's just like God, isn't it?

Last, but not least, I think I speak for all of us in expressing our deepest gratitude for you, the reader. By whatever means, whether you believe it or not, God placed this book in your hands. It is our prayer that He speaks to your heart, gives you peace knowing He is well aware of all things and He has a plan. Perhaps the title compelled you and you need some much-needed biblical guidance for "such a time as this." Whatever the reason, thank you for choosing to spend forty days with familiar stories that, when seen collectively, provide perspective for navigating these uncertain times. May you receive the fullest blessing God intends for you through His Word. Thank you for reading.

# INTRODUCTION

**Navigational Tools**

Those of us who remember traveling before GPS devices were readily accessible may remember this ancient method—asking for directions.

Perhaps some of you are too young to remember this forgotten relic of acquiring the *fastest route* to one's destination, but back in the day, if someone were lost or traveling somewhere new, that traveler would approach someone who seemed to be local—or maybe had the look of a talented navigational scout—and ask them the best route. Though my lifetime intersected this archaic system, I'm not sure how it worked since I'd never ask for directions. Once while traveling to participate in a church service several hours away, my wife (girlfriend then) asked if I knew the directions to which I responded, "How many different churches can there be?" Amazingly, a southern town with a population of 10,000 has lots of churches—enough to make us thirty minutes late, but still, I didn't ask for directions.

Sharing about this old technique increases my appreciation for my GPS, and probably bringing back memories or marital arguments for some of you. Sorry guys.

Even though I never asked for directions, I always carried a map.

Yeah, a paper map, and I wasn't even sailing with Captain Blackbeard—nothing as cool as a treasure map, just one of those road atlases from a Wal-Mart checkout lane.

Yep, I was a map guy.

I was one of the most notorious anti-asking-for- directions-always-had-a map-as-I-traveled-to-speak guys. I was a load of fun on road trips, believe me.

No matter the method—asking directions, maps, backseat driver, printed MapQuest turn by turns, or a GPS—we need help navigating through uncharted territory.

We need help getting where we're going.

We need help to keep us from wasting time circling a town looking for the church where we're supposed to speak as I've done many times.

This navigational help is for traveling from point A to point B, at times to likely important destinations, but not nearly as important as the direction in which we live our lives.

We're all on journeys in life.

We're all having to navigate our way through often uncharted territories.

We don't want to get lost.

We don't want to end up in the wrong place.

We don't want to waste time.

These are the same reasons I ask Siri or the British woman on my GPS for directions these days.

But what do we do for our lives?

What navigational help do we use?

The reason "asking for directions" has fallen by the wayside, and why I haven't bought an updated Road Atlas since 2006, is because GPS devices are so reliable.

A minimum of three sophisticated satellites pinpointing your location and identifying your destination is much more reliable than the most scout-like appearing person at the closest gas station telling you, "I think that's down by the old hardware. Just go down to the light, take a right, or is it left? On second thought just go down to the second light and turn right. Then go down to that road where the green house is and turn right again." A GPS is also much better than trying to squint your eyes to see which little squiggly line you're on and which you need to take.

We turn to a GPS because it's precise and reliable.

The satellites are positioning high above the earth where they can locate the right directions.

When searching for the right path, we should choose a method or resource that's the most trustworthy, right?

So, what about our lives?

Shouldn't we choose the most reliable resource?

Sure, we should. So, what are you using today to navigate your life?

## Uncertain Times

We've always needed help navigating our lives, but as we write *For Uncertain Times* the times are certainly uncertain.

COVID-19 cases are spiking the highest they've been in the United States.

The country is beginning to shut back down.

There's a debate as to the best course of action, and people are hurting financially because of the shutdowns.

Many churches remained closed and debate rage on choosing the right course of action.

A vaccine is beginning to roll out.

There's further debate on whether the vaccine is safe enough.

The most recent presidential election results are being contested, and the nation is divided. There's uncertainty on what will happen next—and which course of action to take.

The Covid-19 pandemic has produced more uncertainty than anything in my life, and maybe for you as well.

All these things are impacting our jobs, pocketbooks, livelihoods, health, and causing many other challenges.

We're in uncertain times.

These days are challenging to navigate.

By the time you read this perhaps that pandemic has passed, but another life-challenging issue will likely surface—if it hasn't already—on a national, state, local, or personal level.

These uncertain times are tricky to traverse, especially for Christ-followers pursuing faithfulness, because Scripture warns that many will turn away. Research shows that most turn away when believers face difficulties, especially challenges they are unprepared to encounter.

Times are certainly uncertain.

How do we faithfully live in them?

What course of action do we take, and how do we choose the right path?


## Been There Before

Uncertain times and national distress are nothing new for God's people. Throughout the ages, God's people have faced such times. They've passed through faithfully and often failed. Their stories are told within the Bible.

Within Scripture, we find not only God's instruction on how to live in difficult days, but we also see many examples of God's people at times they faced trials, especially on a national level.

We began this introduction by discussing where we turn and what resources we use to find reliable direction. This is a point of contention within modern Christianity. Amid this distress, there's much being said in the name of Biblical advice, but very little is being said about the historical examples found in Scripture of God's people in national distress.

Scripture gives us countless instances where God's people faced tough times from oppressive governments. We believe these historical records, and the Bible, allows us to see the choices God's people made, how they lived, and how they should have lived through national distress. We also see how God cared for His people in those uncertain times.

Like the GPS mentioned earlier, the truths we learn from God's people as they lived during national distress should be the most reliable direction and encouragement for our own trying times.

Trying times can be tough to navigate, but we can navigate them with confidence. That's what is before you in this study, in the form of daily devotionals.

You're heading into a 40-day journey that will provide you with trustworthy instruction from Scripture on how to navigate these times so you can continue to live faithfully, with confidence, even as the world turns upside down or completely crazy.

**Welcome from Jake**

I can't thank you enough for choosing *For Uncertain Times*. I'm excited for you in two ways.

First, I know we've presented solid Biblical instruction and encouragement for you in these times. We all need something solid to stand on right now. I'm thankful you've chosen to take this journey with us, to build a strong foundation for uncertain times.

Second, I'm excited you've chosen this as your daily devotional book. The publishing industry has tried to discourage me from publishing my work in the form of devotional books. Instead, they've encouraged me to publish *regular* books. However, I've chosen to go against the grain, to push back. I believe the best thing we can do to thrive amid national distress, and live faithfully every day regardless of our circumstances, is through a regular, daily time with God. This is written to help you to do that. This is not just something for you to do for forty days, but a forty-day jumpstart to building a life-long daily habit.

Over the last several years, I've purchased a handful of devotional books. With each one, I committed the time frame for which they were written. In those times with the Lord, He moved in my life. Each shifted my trajectory closer to where He wanted me. That gives me joy. That makes the effort worth it. Forty days is almost long enough to form a solid habit. Thank you for trusting me enough to choose *For Uncertain Times* and thank you for allowing me to have a part in your daily devotional life. I'm thankful you're going to build a habit of spending regular time with God during uncertain times.

The forty devotions ahead are simply the retelling of stories from Scripture about God's people in difficult times and how God cared for them. We can learn so much with just even a peek into their journeys and God's responses. When you finish, I believe you'll have developed biblical confidence for navigating these trying days. Will you take this forty-day journey and gain instruction for uncertain times?

Again, I've been blessed to partner with Rita Halter Thomas. Rita has years of experience in journalism and writing in general. She's a writer. I'm more of an idea guy. We've collaborated with every book I've written including *Spiritual Prepper* and *Invincible*. She's gracious to combine it all in one voice.

**Welcome from Rita**

What a great honor it is to work with my friend and former pastor, Jake McCandless, on *For Uncertain Times*. As Jake mentioned, it's a great follow-up to our last book, *Invincible,* which fell nicely behind *Spiritual Prepper.*

From working with Jake on his first book, I realized not only the importance of Stand Firm Ministries but the need and urgency of its core message: holding on and standing firm in the faith, especially when believers face their most vulnerable crises. Without a doubt, every page is prayed over, Spirit-lead, and biblical.

Something compelled you to pick up this book. Maybe you are seeking answers or guidance because of the uncertainty in your life, or in our world right now. Maybe the cover grabbed your attention and you just couldn't put it down. Maybe someone gave it to you

Don't get me wrong, whatever the reason resulted in your possession of this book, we're grateful. However, we believe, by whatever means, God placed this book in your hands. It is our prayer that He speaks to your heart, gives you peace knowing He is well aware, and He has a plan. Perhaps you chose this book unaware that God may be calling you to something for "such a time as this."

**Spiritual Prepper Resource**

We call this devotional book a spiritual preparedness resource. Hopefully, you've read my book, *Spiritual Prepper.* If not, I hope you choose to do so. In summary, it picks up the warning in Matthew 24:10, that many will turn away and warns that "anyone" could be any one of us. We're not even in the prophetic time referenced in this verse, but many are turning away, and these uncertain times will grow in frequency and intensity.

I wrote *Spiritual Prepper* to warn of this danger and call readers to spiritually prepare. Just as a doomsday prepper preps for physical danger, we should prepare for the spiritual battles that lie ahead. Instead of building bunkers, stocking up on food, and storing ammunition, we need to be growing closer to our Lord. We need to learn how we should live in uncertain times, and we need to develop a consistent daily routine of spending time with the Lord. We must do these things if we hope to spiritually survive the onslaught of attacks against our faith and our Lord.

*For Uncertain Times*, and the spiritual preparedness resources that follow it, are intended as tools to help you prepare.

## Time for Certainty

Again, thank you for selecting *For Uncertain Times* and for making this forty-day commitment. We've worked hard to give you a tool that provides Biblical instruction for uncertain times. It's important to us because so much is at stake. We pray you will let the Lord speak through the stories we selected that best illustrate how He cared for His people in difficult times. It is our heart's desire these next forty days help prepare you **FOR UNCERTAIN TIMES.**

Week 1

# DISTRESS IN
# EGYPT

# INTRODUCTION
# DISTRESS IN EGYPT

**Uncertain times** came for God's people, the nation of Israel, at the hand of the Egyptians in 15th Century B.C. Israel was heavily oppressed, the people enslaved and forced by Pharaoh into intense labor. He used them for the grunt work of building many of the great monuments along the Nile.

The Israelites came to Egypt as welcomed guests. They were living in Canaan, the land promised to them in the covenant God made with their patriarch Abraham. Jacob, also known as Israel and the chosen son of Isaac, inherited this promised land. That inheritance also extended to Jacob's twelve sons. The families of these sons would become what is commonly known today as the twelve tribes of Israel. We pick up the beginning of their story in Genesis 37, where we see the sons' jealousy of Jacob's favorite, Joseph. That jealousy led them to sell Joseph as a slave and he ended up in Egypt.

Though the eleven jealous brothers acted in cruelty, God was at work. While in prison in Egypt, Joseph interpreted a dream of Pharaoh. This dream was that there would be seven years of plenty and then seven years of famine. Pharaoh, the king of Egypt, was so impressed he made Joseph second-in-command and in charge of preparing for this famine.

When famine struck, it wasn't limited to Egypt, but also affected Canaan. Jacob and his eleven remaining sons and their families were in

3

trouble. Desperate, Joseph's brothers traveled to Egypt in hope for food. There they were reunited with Joseph. What they intended for harm by selling their little brother into slavery, God used for good. God sent Joseph ahead to eventually save his family.

Acknowledging them as family to Joseph, Pharaoh invited Jacob and all his family to move to Egypt so they could survive the famine. They were welcomed guests and even after the famine had passed, the nation (descendants) of Israel stayed. There's debate as to how long they were in Egypt, but it could have been up to four-hundred years. Regardless of the number of their years in Egypt, the Israelites entered with approximately one-hundred and fifty people. We read in Genesis 46 that there were seventy descendants of Jacob that went to Egypt and the chapter tells us that the wives weren't counted. That group of one hundred and fifty had grown to as many as two million at the time when they fell under national distress.

This blessing of God to grow the nation brought trouble. As the Israelites grew in number, Pharaoh worried that they'd grow as large as his nation.

Their supernatural growth made them no longer welcomed guests, but a threat. Therefore, Pharaoh enslaved them.

To slow down the growth of Israel he also ordered the Egyptian midwives to kill Israelite male babies. Pharaoh also continued to intensify the workload of God's people.

Israel faced oppression.

They faced dire times.

This oppression was heavy-handed, so severe that the memory remained in their collective minds for generations to come. It was so oppressive that their time in bondage continues to this day to serve as an illustration of the bonds of sin in one's life and our need for a Savior.

Times were difficult.

Times were uncertain.

What was God's people to do?

What would God do?

What was learned by God's people in this time stood as lessons for them for ages to come. These lessons still serve us today.

What can we learn to help us stand firm in national distress?

What can we learn of God to help us in times of chaos and difficulty?

# 1

## IN UNCERTAIN TIMES
# CHECK YOUR TICKET

*From Genesis 45*
*Drawn from the oppression God's people faced from the*
*Egyptians.*

# THEN

Have you ever been at a movie, ball game, play, or any event that required a ticket and been told you were in someone else's seat?

You know, you check your ticket and see the row and seat number. You search for that row and seat. You sit down and get comfortable and then someone else is standing in front of you or beside you looking down at their ticket and then looking at you saying, "You're in my seat!"

I've been there multiple times.

And when this would happen, I'd check my ticket. Sometimes I was in the wrong seat and other times the other person had misread their ticket. I must confess, a few times I knew I was in the wrong seat but played dumb.

When I think about the situation the Israelites found themselves in during the 15th Century, I often wonder if they were where they were supposed to be.

We referenced their situation in the Week 1 Intro – Egypt, but, in short, the Israelites were enslaved by the Egyptians because they posed a threat to Pharaoh and the nation. Pharaoh forced them to carry out the major building projects. Pharaoh ordered every male Israelite baby to be killed by an Egyptian midwife. The enslavement and oppression were extremely difficult.

Let's remember, the Israelites came to Egypt by invitation. The Pharaoh at that time invited them to live in the nation so they'd survive the great famine. At the time we pick up the story in Exodus, they'd been in Egypt for possibly 400 years.

Egypt wasn't the land of their inheritance—Canaan was their inheritance. It had been promised to Abraham and his descendants—the Israelites.

So, were they where God wanted them to be?

Were they in His will?

They needed to check their ticket.

They needed to reflect on the instruction, directions, calling, and mission God had given them.

I can't say with any factual evidence that they were supposed to be in Egypt at that point. I just believe the answer to be yes. If they "checked their ticket" they'd find two things.

First, they'd find clarity that their initial arrival in Egypt had been by the will of the Lord. In Genesis 45, Joseph finally reveals his identity to his brothers who'd traveled to Egypt for food. When Joseph did this his brothers were terrified, for they knew their guilt— and Joseph's authority to punish them. But quickly Joseph reassured them that what had happened was God's will. God had sent him ahead so that when the famine came the whole family would be saved. He went on to say in verse 6-8, "For two years now there has been famine in the land, and for the next five years there will be no plowing and reaping. But God sent me ahead of you to preserve for you a remnant on earth and to save your lives by a great deliverance. So then, it was not you who sent me here, but God. He made me father to Pharaoh, lord of his entire household and ruler of all Egypt."

Joseph was certain God's will was for his family to move to Egypt. This seems to be confirmed through his family and through Pharaoh inviting them to live in the land of Goshen.

So, although difficulty had arisen, it didn't change the fact that they went exactly where God led them.

Checking their "ticket," they'd see they were in the right "seat". However, they also needed to reflect on what God promised their great patriarchs—Abraham and Isaac.

The second thing they would find—if they were able to have taken a comprehensive look at all God had told them—was that Egypt wasn't their final destination. Though they had taken the right steps, they wouldn't stay there. Nor were they meant to stay there.

This should have led them to ask of God, "Is it time to return?" or to fit our theme, "Is this ticket still good?"

# NOW

As you look around and see uncertain times in this nation, or maybe in your own life, you're not the first of God's people to go through tribulation. It just comes with the territory. But what should you do?

Check your ticket.

Yes, check your ticket.

Are you in the place where God led you to be?

This can be a real physical location, but more than likely this question searches the *activity* of your life.

Are you seeking the Lord?

Have you been seeking Him?

Have you been in His Word?

Are you in community with other believers?

Have you been pursuing holiness so that your heart and spiritual eyes aren't compromised?

And the simplest way to check your "ticket" is just to ask the Lord.

Often, you'll see you're in the right seat, but there may be times you walked your own path—you ran ahead of God or did things your own way. If that's the case, seek Him and let Him guide you to the correct seat.

If you find you're in the right seat, *know* it. Difficulties and doubt cause us to second guess what we've heard from the Lord and how to take steps of obedience. Circumstances aren't always an indicator of obedience and being in His Will.

If you're in the right seat, you'll need to weather the storm—ride it out in faith.

Life is full of difficult trials. Even the right path can lead us head-on into them, but there's no need to bring unnecessary difficulty upon ourselves. Heed the words of Solomon in Proverbs: "**Trust in the Lord** with all your heart and lean not on your own understanding; in all your ways submit to him, and he will make your paths straight" (Proverbs 3:5-6, NIV).

# INSTRUCTION FOR UNCERTAIN TIMES:
## CHECK YOUR TICKET

# 2
## IN UNCERTAIN TIMES
# STICK TO YOUR GUNS

*From Exodus 1 - 2*
*Drawn from the oppression God's people faced from the Egyptians*

# THEN

Israel experienced freedom for many years in Egypt, but as the Israelites' numbers grew, that freedom was taken away. You may recall from this weeks' introduction, not only were the Israelites enslaved, but the oppression against them—their labor and difficulties—became heavier and heavier. Pharaoh despised the Israelites.

This hatred toward God's people didn't end with the ten plagues in Egypt. It has continued throughout history—recorded in the Old Testament, New Testament, and through the time since the close of the New Testament to now. God's people have an enemy—Satan. His work on Earth is centered upon destroying the people of God. This is recorded clearly in Revelation 12. Therefore, God's people then and now need to know how to remain faithful and stand firm in the midst of persecution and great oppression like that which Israel faced from Pharaoh. That's the purpose of this devotional book—to help you stand firm.

Not only did Pharaoh attempt to break the people of Israel through difficult labor and conditions, but he also ordered the Hebrew midwives to kill all male babies born to Israel. Eventually, not only were they ordered to be killed, but also to be thrown into the Nile River. Although given this edict from the most powerful man on Earth at that time, the midwives ignored the orders. Exodus 1:17 records that these women feared God, so they didn't carry out the Egyptian king's orders. Though they knew Pharaoh could and probably would kill them, they feared God more. They feared the eternal repercussions more than Pharaoh's punishment.

Reading further in that chapter we learn, due to their faithfulness, God granted them favor. That's not always the case, but in this instance the midwives were protected from harm.

In Exodus 2, we learn of the birth of a specific Hebrew male—Moses. Moses' mother also feared God, and rather than throwing her son into the Nile, she waterproofed a basket and placed her baby in it. She trusted God would take care of her son. Not only did God allow her son to be rescued—he allowed Moses to be rescued by the Pharaoh's daughter. God even arranged for Moses' own mother to be selected to raise him.

Moses' mother and the Israelite midwives stuck to their guns.

We're not told much about how the children of Israel kept their identity and faith in God during this time, but they did. There was a vein of faithfulness in them. They had their distinction as followers of the God of Abraham, Isaac, Jacob, and Joseph.

They stuck to their guns.

They stood firm.

They remained faithful even when the world turned against them and their future seemed hopeless.

# NOW

The idiom "stick to your guns" is used today as an encouragement, or a description of keeping to one's beliefs and/or convictions even when everyone and everything is against us. This phrase originates from the Navy, as a command given to sailors who manned guns on military boats. They were commanded to stay at their posts even when the boat was under attack.

Picture the chaos aboard a battleship under fire from enemy aircraft and enemy warships. Sailors are running all over the ship and fires rage throughout. Among the smoke and gunfire, they struggle even to hear themselves think. The ship could even be taking on water. The fear of sinking would have to weigh heavily on each sailor's mind. Still, they know they must stay at their posts and fire their guns at the enemy—not just fire, but focus with such deliberate concentration that the job is done well and effectively.

No matter what.

No matter the cost.

That's the meaning of the idiom.

It's what the Israelites did when faced with drastic oppression and persecution. It's especially what the midwives did.

Though we may not be on a ship in the middle of an attack—we may be in a chaotic situation in life—if not now, we likely will be. Though we may not be stationed on anti-aircraft guns on the deck of a battleship, we're called to keep the faith, stand firm, and continue on ahead following Christ.

When there's uncertain times in our nation, heck, when there's uncertainty anywhere in our lives, we must stick to our guns.

Considering the Hebrew midwives and how they didn't fear Pharaoh and his wrath, but instead feared God and His wrath, I recall Jesus' words recorded in Matthew: "**Do not be afraid of those who** kill the body but cannot kill the soul. Rather, be afraid of the One who can destroy both soul and body in hell" (Matthew 10:28, NIV). It's this same conviction we need for strength, courage, and this conviction provides motivation to stick and stay when we face great challenges of our faith in chaotic times.

# INSTRUCTION FOR UNCERTAIN TIMES:
## STICK TO YOUR GUNS

# 3
## IN UNCERTAIN TIMES
# BE BRAVE

*From Exodus 1 - 2*
*Drawn from the oppression God's people faced from the Egyptians*

# THEN

Yesterday we looked at how the Israelite midwives and Moses' mother stuck to their guns, as well as the whole nation to some degree. Even in challenging, life-threatening circumstances, they kept their faith and integrity.

I believe the whole nation needs to be commended on how they kept their identity after such a long time in the middle of Egypt. Throughout the Old Testament, prophets were consistently sent to tell Israel to repent from the idolatry of their neighbors and return to God. We see a constant acceptance by Israel of the practices and idolatry of the other nations throughout Scripture. Yet, here in Egypt, they kept their identity. To be fair, there are allusions throughout the Bible, especially in Joshua, indicating some practice of the worship of Egyptian gods, but for the most part, it appears Israel remained faithful to the One True God.

This had to be difficult.

The Hebrew midwives disobeyed Pharaoh's orders because they feared the One True God. They did this at the risk of their lives.

Moses' mother was the same way.

They showed bravery.

17

Though there was distress nationally and, in their lives, they were brave to stand for God and His ways.

Bravery is found throughout the Exodus account, not just here.

Though Moses gave excuses, he sill displayed great courage in returning to Egypt and facing Pharaoh. Aaron displayed this same bravery by going with Moses.

Though the people moan and complain throughout the story of Exodus, it took courage for them to leave Egypt—especially to walk through the parted waters of the Red Sea, witnessing God's power as He dried the ground beneath their feet.

Moses showed bravery in ascending Mount Sinai.

Caleb and Joshua especially showed courage when they returned from their spying endeavor. They saw large, fortified cities and giants in the land but still were ready to fight for the Promised Land. Bravery is especially seen in the conquest of Canaan.

As presented in this book, in all of the seasons where God's people suffer oppression, courage and bravery will be the elements that define them in the middle of desperate times. In trials, God's people have shown bravery.

Scripture indicates God is pleased with courage and bravery. And it's not so much the bravery itself, but the fact that that such bravery comes from an undaunted faith in God.

# NOW

One of the greatest realities presented in Scripture, seen in God's sanctifying work in our lives, is that we should not trust in ourselves or our own strength, but rather trust in Him. God wants us to rely on Him. The best thing for our lives is to give up our own strength and lean on His.

A Christian's courage is never meant to be isolated from faith. Actually, the bravery of a follower of Christ is best described as faith.

So, in any talk of courage, we can't think of it as a characteristic severed from faith in God.

Bravery is a trait that pleases God. When your eyes are open to it as you read the Bible, you'll be shocked at the number of times God's people are called to be courageous and are commended for having courage.

Scripture and experience also teach us that courage is necessary for standing firm in the midst of the chaos in this world.

When times are uncertain, we're to be brave.

It's written repeatedly in the Bible.

The clearest example of this instruction from God's Word is given in relation to the Exodus account. After Moses' death and Joshua's ascension to leadership, before the campaign to conquer Canaan, the Lord tells Joshua to be strong and very courageous. Here's one of these times: **"Be strong and very courageous. Be careful to obey all the law my servant Moses gave you; do not turn from it to the right or to the left, that you may be successful wherever you go. Keep this Book of the Law always on your lips; meditate on it day and night, so that you may be careful to do everything written in it. Then you will be prosperous and successful. Have I not commanded you? Be strong and courageous. Do not be afraid; do not be discouraged, for the Lord your God will be with you wherever you go" (Joshua 1:7-9, NIV).**

Joshua needed to have such courage because he was leading Israel into battle, but we're all called to have such courage. We need it to stand firm when times get tough.

# INSTRUCTION FOR UNCERTAIN TIMES:
## BE BRAVE

# 4
## IN UNCERTAIN TIMES
# CRY OUT TO GOD

*From Exodus 3*
*Drawn from the oppression God's people faced from the Egyptians*

# THEN

Surely, I'm not the only one who's strained my guts out, spent way too much time or worrying far too much while doing something on my own, only to hear from someone afterwards—"why didn't you call on me? I'd have loved to help you." I'm fiercely independent so I do this often. It's stupid when someone could and would help with just a call.

It makes me think of the game show, *Who Wants to Be a Millionaire.* In the show contestants begin with three lifelines, one of which is phoning a friend to help answer a question. It's sad when the contestant tries to answer the question on their own and gets it wrong, when all they needed to do was call a friend.

Why not ask for help?

Why not ask help from God?

While that should be the first thing we do when we're in trouble, often we exhaust all our own efforts before asking God for help.

21

In Exodus 1, we read of the Egyptian taskmasters and their ruthless, brutal treatment of the Israelites, God's people. The Egyptians pressed down hard on the Hebrews, forcing them to build with brick and mortar or work in the fields.

Israel found themselves in a dire situation longing for freedom.

They were oppressed.

They were persecuted.

They didn't have a voice.

They weren't free.

What would they do?

In Exodus 3, when God is speaking to Moses through the burning bush, He calls Moses to ask Pharaoh to release Israel. In this exchange, God states that His people are crying out to Him for help.

At some point Israel cried out to God.

He heard them and He responded.

Exodus 3:7-8 tells that because of their cries, God came down and rescued them.

They were right to cry out to God when in their difficult position.

# NOW

Nothing has changed in God's relationship with His people. In Paul's letter to the Romans, he explains that Gentile Christ-followers were grafted into Israel. Therefore, all the promises God made to the Israelites are true for us today. How God interacted with them then is how He interacts with us today.

And when they were in the calamity of enslavement in Egypt, they cried out to God and He heard.

Therefore, when we are facing a trial, or our world has been turned upside down, we too should cry out and God will hear us. He will hear. He will respond in the way that is best for our lives.

If you're like me, then you'll be tempted to exhaust all your efforts and resources before crying out (praying) to God for help, but why not start with petitioning the One who can do all things?

There's nothing fancy or religious that has to be said when "crying out." Simply, talk to God. Tell Him your situation (of course, He already knows). Ask him for help. Be specific. Not that He needs that information, but He wants us to realize we're nothing apart from Him.

Cry out.

Pray.

Call out to Him.

That's it. It's that easy.

What Israel did when they were facing tribulation in Egypt, is what Paul also told the believers in Rome. He was writing about salvation from our sins, but many examples and teachings in Scripture would support that the truth of this passage extends to all areas of our lives. Paul wrote: **"Everyone who calls on the name of the Lord will be saved" (Romans 10:13, NIV).**

# INSTRUCTION FOR UNCERTAIN TIMES: CRY OUT TO GOD

# 5
## IN UNCERTAIN TIMES
# GOD HEARS OUR CRIES

*From Exodus 1 - 2*
*Drawn from the oppression God's people faced from the Egyptians*

# THEN

Yesterday on our drive back from church, I heard the distinctive sound of my youngest daughter punch my oldest daughter in the face. It's not a surprise, for my youngest has an anger problem like the Incredible Hulk, only she turns red, not green. And my oldest has a knack for aggravating my youngest. Regardless of the repetitiveness of the aggravating, my youngest mustn't hit—no matter who started it.

Of course, when asked why she hit her sister, my daughter said it is because her sister took something. To which I responded: "no matter what your sister has done you can't punch her. You need to tell me or Mom that she took something." Then I pronounced the punishment that would ensue.

And my youngest began crying, but she wasn't upset about the upcoming punishment. She was upset because she had told me ten times that her older sister had taken something, but I had not heard. I wanted to immediately defend my case, but I believe she was telling the truth. I was too engaged in conversation with my wife or in listening to the game on the radio, I didn't hear my daughter's cry for help. In my defense, this event transpires nearly daily.

In yesterday's devotional we looked at how in Exodus 3:7 the Israelites cried out to God for help. We also looked at how that this is what God wants of His people—to rely on Him. But in that same verse, God says He has heard their cries and He has seen their misery. So, not only did the people cry out, but God heard them. The Lord said, "I have indeed seen the misery of my people in Egypt. I have heard them crying out because of their slave drivers, and I am concerned about their suffering" (Exodus 3:7).

Though the answer was a response for the cries of God's people, even before they cried out to Him, He saw their plight. So, why didn't He come sooner? I don't know. God has His own timing. We must trust He knows best.

I believe it's important to know that He sees what we're facing.

There's also something to be said about Him answering when we cry out. Throughout the Bible there are teachings on asking Him for what we need. God knows, but still He calls on us to ask. At the same time, though God is Sovereign, He responds when we ask.

# NOW

God's eyes and ears haven't changed in the nearly 3,500 years since the Exodus. Like how He responded to Israel's cries in Egypt, He'll respond to us in our struggles.

As mentioned above in this situation there is the question of why God waited on them to cry out to respond. Why did He wait? I don't know.

Although we can't definitively answer the question, we can follow the example of God's people. When in trouble—cry out to God. When in need—cry out to God. And when you do, He hears.

Also, it's a comfort that He saw their misery. God sees and cares about the details of our lives. One of the most comforting passages in the Bible, to me, is found in Matthew 10:29-31: "**Are not two sparrows sold for a penny? Yet not one of them will fall to the ground outside your Father's care. And even the very hairs of your head are all numbered. So don't be afraid; you are worth more than many sparrows" (Matthew 10:29-31, NIV).**

God hears when we cry out to Him, but He also already knows. He knows what *big* thing is going on in your life because He cares about the *little* things in your life, like the numbers of hairs on your head.

# INSTRUCTION FOR UNCERTAIN TIMES: GOD HEARS OUR CRIES

# 6

IN UNCERTAIN TIMES
# GOD ALREADY HAS A PLAN

*From Exodus 3*
*Drawn from the oppression God's people faced from the Egyptians*

## THEN

"What ifs" can be killers if we reflect on them, especially when looking back on a tragedy or great loss. In our analysis of God's response to His people while they were oppressed in Egypt, there are "what ifs." He heard and responded to their cries. He rescued them. But Exodus 3:7 indicates that He saw their misery even before they cried out. So, why didn't He respond? Why did He even have to wait to see it happen, when He knew what was going to happen? Why allow His people to go through such trials if He was going to rescue them anyway?

Obviously, we know that God used the slavery in Egypt and especially the rescue in huge way in shaping His people and their understanding of Him.

But we also must realize that God's response to rescue had been in the works eighty years before it manifested.

Moses' preservation at birth.

Moses being found by the Pharaoh's daughter.

Moses being raised in the palace.

Moses' mother being able to lay a foundation in his life.

The forty years in the wilderness.

All of these events led to Moses being ready to lead the people how God wanted.

Often, we may feel that God isn't responding, isn't swooping in to rescue us, when all the while, He is, and has been working behind the scenes on the rescue. God is always to be trusted.

In everything that happened to God's people in Egypt and in the Exodus out of Egypt, lessons were taught, and shaping which continued for centuries was accomplished. Events of the last days even connect back to this time, with Jesus' return marking a second Exodus. God is the master author, and He is writing a masterpiece. We must trust Him.

For the sake of His people, God responded.

Even before His response was visible to them, He had been working at least eighty years.

Also, God's responses are very tangible.

They're earthy.

In Exodus 3:8, we read that God came down to save His people. And there's no doubt that His supernatural acts were what set the enslaved nation free, but God chose to raise up and send out Moses to be a visual savior. God used real-life means to rescue His people.

# NOW

When life is out of control and times are uncertain, know that if God seems silent this doesn't mean He's not working behind the scenes—He likely is working good.

He is the master author and playwright.

He can be trusted.

Also look for real-life answers to your prayers.

Yes, God does supernatural acts. He commits miracles, but far more than that, He uses real, down-to-earth methods to respond to His people.

Yes, the Angel of the Lord would've been more effective than Moses, but God chose to use Moses. He does this all through-out history. One of the reasons that God's people didn't realize Jesus was the Messiah was because their expectations were beyond real life. Jesus was too tangible; He was too real.

Know that if you cry out to God, He'll respond.

And it's highly likely He's already has His plan in motion.

**"And we know that in all things God works for the good of those who love him, who have been called according to his purpose" (Romans 8:28, NIV).**

# INSTRUCTION FOR UNCERTAIN TIMES: GOD ALREADY HAS A PLAN

# 7
## IN UNCERTAIN TIMES
# GOD CARES FOR HIS PEOPLE

*From Exodus 11 – Joshua 1*
*Drawn from the oppression God's people faced from the Egyptians*

# THEN

This book is the second of our Spiritual Preparedness Devotional Books. In the first book, *Invincible*, we looked at how when God calls His people to a task or mission, He takes care of them. He gives them victory, provides, and protects. The hope was to help readers build up their confidence in God. *For Uncertain Times* does much of the same, except it focuses on specific instances of when God's people faced turmoil.

As we sought accounts of God's victories, provision, and protection in the Bible, we repeatedly were drawn to the Exodus account. We weren't the first to be drawn back to that watershed event; almost every prophet and Biblical writer also referenced Israel back to that time. We should continually return to this pivotal series of events for it shows God liberating His people who were enslaved by the mightiest kingdom of the day. It shows God being victorious over all other lesser gods and over all elements of nature.

Even more, God sustained up to two million people in a barren land. God gave them a path through the Red Sea when there was no way. God defeated the powerful army of Egypt in one swoop. He sent them pillars of fire and cloud that guided their path and timing. He provided water in supernatural ways. The same was done with food. He did this for over 40 years.

When they needed water, God turned a lake of bitter water into drinkable water by having Moses throw in a log. He provided water from a rock by having Moses strike it. He later would provide water by having Moses speak to a rock. Daily food was provided by a mysterious substance called manna that fell each day. When the people complained of the diet of manna, God sent an abundance of quail, so much so, that the two million people had so much to eat they grew sick.

Israel's guide in the wilderness, the pillar of cloud and fire, showed the people when to go and stay. It showed them where to go. God provided for every need they had. He took care of His people in the wilderness. In one of the most treacherous parts of the world, they were without want.

Though in many ways Israel had been led out of their oppression, when it came to their wilderness time, this wilderness sojourn was part of the process. Process may be the key word. Israel's rescue from their first captivity began at least eighty years before the event occurred. It continued for months and eventually years due to the disobedience of the people. The process involved preparing a rescuer, executing the rescue, sending plagues, providing for the journey with the Egyptians handing over their own goods, parting of the Red Sea, destruction of the Egyptian Army, a wilderness journey, wilderness provision, the giving of the Law at Mount Sinai, and many more challenges in the wilderness.

# NOW

More than likely, with any work of God in your life, especially while times are uncertain, there will be a process. We want quick fixes, but often God uses a process. We don't want to endure a process, but that's what we need.

One of the most remarkable verses about the Exodus is found in Exodus 19:4, "You yourselves have seen what I did to Egypt, and how I carried you on eagles' wings and brought you to myself" (Exodus 19:4, NIV).

Did you catch what this is saying?

When we think of the Exodus, we think the purpose was to rescue Israel for the sake of their freedom and betterment. But the Promised Land, though a blessing to them and for them, wasn't the best for them. God was the best for them. His process wasn't just about getting them rescued, it was about bringing them to Him.

That's still how God works.

God isn't just working in our lives to make our lives better for our enjoyment, though the byproduct is just that. He knows the best for us is in Him. So, in His workings, He will use a process. That process may leave us feeling that we've been led out to a barren wasteland. It's highly likely that is the case, but in that process, in that wilderness of the soul and reality, He will care for us like He did for Israel.

One of the comforting verses for His people throughout history and true today is found in Psalm 91. The language alludes to the passage above from Exodus 19:4. He told Israel He carried them on "eagles' wings" then. And the Psalmist possibly reflecting on this encourages the reader with that same type promise. **He will cover you with his feathers, and under his wings you will find refuge; his faithfulness will be your shield and rampart" (Psalm 91:4, NIV).**

# INSTRUCTION FOR UNCERTAIN TIMES:
## GOD CARES FOR HIS PEOPLE

Week 2

# DISTRESS IN
# ASSYRIA

Week 2
# INTRODUCTION
# DISTRESS IN ASSYRIA

**Uncertain times** fell on God's people, the twelve tribes of Israel, again in the 8th century, at the hand of an army which history calls the cruelest to ever exist. This force belonged to the Assyrians. Ten of the Israelite tribes were driven out of the land and displaced. Two tribes remained but faced a perilous siege.

In fairness to history and the Word, there were only a few years in the History of Israel that were *certain* and free from national-level strife. The times mentioned in this book highlight the most challenging they faced. At the time of the Assyrian campaigns, the Kingdom of Israel had been split in two. Ten tribes made up the northern half, named Israel, with its capital in Samaria. The Southern Kingdom, comprised of the tribes of Judah and Benjamin, became known as Judah. For much of Assyria's height of power, its capital was Nineveh, located in modern-day Iraq. Assyria sought to expand its territory and needed Israel for its main trade route and access to the Mediterranean Sea.

When the threat from Nineveh first arose, King Ahab of the Northern Kingdom led a coalition of nations against them. These campaigns brought temporary relief, but eventually the Northern Kingdom of Israel became an Assyrian vassal state and was forced to pay an annual tribute. As a vassal state the oppression upon them was minimal, but the threat of the growing power in the far north loomed.

During this time, prophets like Amos, Hosea, and Micah warned the people of the Northern Kingdom if they refused to turn from idolatry and back to God, He'd exile them from the land. At this same time, the prophet Isaiah warned the Southern Kingdom of Judah.

Near 725 B.C., Israel's King Hoshea rebelled and withheld their tribute which caused the Assyrians to put Samaria under siege for three years. In 722 B.C., Samaria fell and the Northern Kingdom was driven from the land.

Twenty-one years after destroying Samaria, the Assyrian king, Sennacherib, led a campaign into Judah. In this campaign, he destroyed forty-six cities. Almost all of the major cities, except the capital, Jerusalem, fell.

Sennacherib then marched on Jerusalem, surrounding it with 185,000 soldiers. Judah's king, Hezekiah, prepared Jerusalem as much as possible to survive the siege. He reinforced the fortifications, stored great amounts of food, and dug a tunnel to the Gihon Spring outside the city—Hezekiah's tunnel can be seen today. He also prepared Judah's army and made attempts to align with Egypt and Babylon—attempts that failed.

Attempts that the prophet warned King Hezekiah against making.

All the efforts fail short.

King Hezekiah and the people of Jerusalem were in trouble.

All other major cities had fallen.

A large army surrounded them.

This army had already laid waste to the entire Levant—and done so with great cruelty.

God's people in Judah had watched the Northern Kingdom be destroyed and everyone exiled. They heard the reports of the destruction of all the other cities in their own nation.

The siege raged on.

This was a time of great distress. Imagine the 185,000 soldiers encamped around them, ready to scale the walls and ransack the city. Dire.

The distress—the near annihilation of the people of God—left Judah to face difficult times at the hands of the Assyrians.

Times were difficult.

Times were uncertain.

What were God's people to do?

What would God do?

What was learned by God's people in this time stood as lessons for them for ages to come. These lessons still serve us today.

What can we learn to help us stand firm in national distress?

What can we learn of God that will help us in times of chaos and difficulty?

# 8

# GOD HAS BEEN PATIENT

*From Isaiah 30 & 31, 2 Kings 18-19*
*Drawn from the Assyrian attack, siege, and exile of God's people.*

## THEN

As we shared in the Week 2 intro, the destruction of Samaria in 722 B.C. resulted in the exile of Israel—a devastating and horrifying time for God's people. Make no bones about it, God allowed this to take place. The prophet Isaiah explained the role of Assyria, "Woe to the Assyrian, the rod of my anger, in whose hand is the club of my wrath! I send him against a godless nation, I dispatch him against a people who anger me, to seize loot and snatch plunder, and to trample them down like mud in the streets" (Isaiah 10:5-6, NIV). Through Isaiah, God says that Assyria's conquest was allowed by God to be wrath or punishment for Israel's idolatry and unfaithfulness to Him.

When we read about the terrible event and understand that God allowed it, a common question comes to mind. Why does God allow bad things to happen? After all, He's a loving God. He proclaims it, as does His people. On the surface, this seems like a fair question, but the event in 722 B.C. was not a spur-of-the-moment occurrence. God exercised patience through Israel's disobedience for at least 700 years before the invasion, and especially for the 200 years previous to it.

Keep in mind in 2020, the United States is only 244 years old, and it has only been about 500 years since Columbus discovered the Americas.

The entrance into the Promised Land at the time of Moses and Joshua happened around 1400 B.C. Before heading into this land and Joshua assuming leadership, Moses gathered the Israelites and retold the Law, as recorded in Deuteronomy. Along with the Law, stipulations applied. If Israel obeyed the Law and remained faithful to God, then the Israelites could live in the land and enjoy it. But if they disobeyed Him and worshipped idols, they would be removed from the land. These were the conditions of the Mosaic Covenant.

God blessed and Israel entered and inhabited the land, but not long into their tenure, they began to turn from God and toward idols. This continued. The Book of Judges, which tells of this time, provides an account of repeated cycles of disobedience. The Israelites disobeyed. God sent a judge or prophet to set them straight. They repented, only to suffer a repeat of the same cycle.

This stipulation was set 700 years before the Assyrian victory.

In 930 B.C., the kingdom split. When the ten tribes formed their own kingdom, they also formed their own "religion." They worshiped idols. This sin continued for 200 years. Rather than heed the warnings of their prophets, they killed the prophets. For 200 years, they perverted the law of God. For 200 years, they grossly worshipped idols.

Yes, God allowed Assyria to exile His people, but He showed patience for 700 years, and particularly the 200 years of the Northern Kingdom's existence. God also exercised patience with the Southern Kingdom for yet another 200 years.

All of which is evidence that God is patient.

Even before trouble befell His people, God was patient. And if they humbled themselves and repented, His patience continued.

# NOW

The Bible gives us further evidence of God's patience, not just the handling of His people at the hands of the Assyrians. He tells us throughout the Bible, especially in 2 Peter 3: "**The Lord is not slow in keeping his promise, as some understand slowness. Instead he is patient with you, not wanting anyone to perish, but everyone to come to repentance" (2 Peter 3:9, NIV).**

This is the character of God. He is patient.

So, when it thunders in your life as a result of sin, know up front that God has been patient with you for some time. Think beyond the uncertainty to all that preceded it. Also know, if the distress is due to sin, you must humble yourself and repent. God is still patient.

You must also know, regardless of the cause of distress, when you turn and seek God, He will be patient. That's who He is.

## INSTRUCTION FOR UNCERTAIN TIMES: GOD HAS BEEN PATIENT

# 9
# IN UNCERTAIN TIMES
# GOD WARNS

*From Isaiah 30 & 31, 2 Kings 18-19*
*Drawn from the Assyrian attack, siege, and exile of God's people.*

# THEN

In the 200 years from inception to demise, the ten northern tribes of Israel were continually warned to leave the practice of idolatry and return to God. They were warned to repent, or they'd be exiled. It was a warning first relayed to God's people through Moses 700 years before exile occurred:

> *For I command you today to love the Lord your God,*
> *to walk in obedience to him, and to keep his commands,*
> *decrees and laws; then you will live and increase, and*
> *the Lord your God will bless you in the land you are*
> *entering to possess. But if your heart turns away and you*
> *are not obedient, and if you are drawn away to bow*
> *down to other gods and worship them, I declare to you*
> *this day that you will certainly be destroyed. You will not*

*live long in the land you are crossing the Jordan to enter and possess* (Deuteronomy 30:16-18, NIV).

This was a long-standing warning, but God continually sent prophets to warn Israel that their sin was leading them to destruction. Amos was sent to relay this warning, "You only have I chosen of all the families of the earth; therefore I will punish you for all your sins" (Amos 3:2, NIV). "I abhor the pride of Jacob and detest his fortresses; I will deliver up the city and everything in it" (Amos 6:8, NIV). Amos' warning to the nation came 40 years before the invasion. The people still had a chance to repent and change their fate.

God led the prophet Hosea to live out an illustration by marrying a prostitute, Gomer. Hosea's wife consistently left him, and, in each instance, he would buy her back. Imagine the humiliation. The Lord had Hosea do this to show the adulterous idolatry of Israel and the faithfulness of God. Hosea also was given a message to warn the people that judgment was coming.

Recorded in Hosea, "When the Lord began to speak through Hosea, the Lord said to him, 'Go, marry a promiscuous woman and have children with her, for like an adulterous wife this land is guilty of unfaithfulness to the Lord'" (Hosea 1:2, NIV). "She conceived and bore him a son. Then the Lord said to Hosea, 'Call him Jezreel, because I will soon punish the house of Jehu for the massacre at Jezreel, and I will put an end to the kingdom of Israel'" (Hosea 1:3b-4, NIV). Hosea's unique message was given up to 30 years before the destruction of Samaria.

Micah warned Israel immediately before the exile. "Therefore I will make Samaria a heap of rubble…" (Micah 1:6a, NIV). "All this is because of Jacob's transgression, because of the sins of the people of Israel" (Micah 1:5, NIV).

These are the three main prophets who warned the Northern Kingdom immediately before the exile, but there were others. Elijah and Elisha gave the same warnings.

While Assyria was wiping out the northern tribes, Isaiah warned Judah that if they didn't remain faithful the same would happen to them.

God warned His people that distress was coming upon the nation. He gave ample warning.

# NOW

God's people didn't always—nearly never—respond to His warnings, but they were warned. The Lord didn't owe it to them, but He did warn them. In every instance of national distress that came upon the people of God, He warned them.

Today in Christianity there's a spectrum of varying views about how prophecy works. I believe this confusion is dangerous, but there is a Biblical bridge that supports God providing a warning of future events without dealing with the views of the gift of prophecy. How? Every believer is indwelt by the Holy Spirit and, in the Gospel of John, Jesus says that the Holy Spirit would be a guide: **"But when he, the Spirit of truth, comes, he will guide you into all the truth...and he will tell you what is yet to come" (John 16:13, NIV).** I believe it's safe to assume that a Divine Guide wouldn't merely guide directionally, but also would guide us concerning time. Did you catch the last phrase in the verse, "he will tell you what is yet to come?"

The Holy Spirit is able to tell us what is to come.

Regardless how He does it or will do it, God warns.

We need to be in tune with Him, the Holy Spirit, to hear guidance.

We must also be in tune with Him and grounded in the Word so we can discern prophetic warnings that God may be giving us through others.

# INSTRUCTION FOR UNCERTAIN TIMES:
## GOD WARNS

# 10

# GOD COULD BE PUNISHING SIN

*From Isaiah 30 & 31, 2 Kings 18-19*
*Drawn from the Assyrian attack, siege, and exile of God's people.*

## THEN

So far, we've been learning how God interacted with His people, and how His people responded as a nation when faced with chaos and oppression. The purpose is to translate all we learn into our lives as we face trials and tribulations. To do this we must look at specific actions in the Scriptural accounts of events that provide the best examples, so understand the selection is far from exhaustive. Other details from the events are left out. However, in this week's focus on the Assyrian invasion, and in next week's focus on the Babylonian invasion, there is a reality that cannot be overlooked even if it doesn't fit into our theme and flow. Not addressing that reality—that Biblical principle—would be mishandling the Scriptures. Let's get to it.

Israel's destruction at the hands of Assyria and the later exile of Judah by the Babylonians were direct consequences or punishments for personal and corporate sin. This wasn't the case with the oppression in

53

Egypt. Egyptian pressure was a matter of circumstances. Circumstances beyond our control create some serious uncertainty in our lives, and that reality is unsettling. All difficulty stems from the sin of Adam and Eve in the Garden, but not all trials in our lives are a direct consequence for—or discipline of— our own sins.

Jesus addressed this subject in Luke 13:1-5. He commented on two recent tragedies in the nation. The first tragedy happened to a group of Galileans who were killed as a result of the Roman governor using force. The second was an incident where a tower or scaffolding fell at Siloam and killed eighteen people. In that day the common view was that these people died because they'd sinned, but Jesus stresses the people involved weren't killed because of their sin. Rather, their deaths were merely due to unfortunate life circumstances and, in a fallen world, these things happen.

God used the prophets ahead of the invasion to point out the coming events weren't merely coincidental life circumstances; rather, the invasion was a result of Israel's unfaithfulness—Israel's sin. The exilic prophets like Daniel, Jeremiah, and Ezekiel were called by God to tell the children of Judah they were exiled to Babylon because of their sin.

God made it clear why tragedy came upon them.

Understanding that the Assyrian invasion resulted from sin still doesn't clarify the needed point from Scripture. What is clearly presented from all the warnings of the prophets and the retelling of the historic events is that God *hates* sin.

Whether it's thematic or not, we would fail you and the Word to omit the most evident principle in this major moment of the Assyrian invasion: God abhors sin and will deal with it. His hatred for sin hasn't changed.

# NOW

Your difficulties in life could be due to unfortunate life circumstances—even in most cases. I am confident saying this because I face unfortunate circumstances ranging from the inconvenient to the tragic all the time. But that's not to say God doesn't punish or discipline us. He refers to Assyria as his rod of wrath (paddle for us today). If you believe your difficulty may be due to your sin—ask! Ask the Lord! His shoulders are big enough to handle the question. That is the point of His discipline; it is to bring us back to Him, and back to a restored relationship with Him.

Seriously take this truth into account and seek the reason for your tribulation, but don't dwell on it too long, as Job and his friends did in the Book of Job. The Holy Spirit will reveal to you if your struggles come as punishment, but more likely your trials are circumstances of this fallen-world-life.

This truth of uncertain times resulting from sin isn't limited to our personal trials but particularly extends to nations as a whole. The warnings given from the prophets were speaking of the punishment coming on the nation corporately.

Even so, in trying times or not, the bottom-line truth we must understand is that God hates sin.

Therefore, repent.

Leave that sin in the dust.

Recorded early in the Book of Acts is the response the Apostle Peter gives the crowd after God heals a lame man through Peter, he said, **"Repent, then, and turn to God, so that your sins may be wiped out, that times of refreshing may come from the Lord" (1 John 1:9, NIV).**

# INSTRUCTION FOR UNCERTAIN TIMES:
## GOD COULD BE PUNISHING SIN

# 11
## IN UNCERTAIN TIMES
# GOD WILL PULL THE TRIGGER

*From Isaiah 30 & 31, 2 Kings 18-19*
*Drawn from the Assyrian attack, siege, and exile of God's people.*

# THEN

As we read in the previous devotional, God warns His people of what is to come. He warned Israel and Judah of the Assyrian invasion. The warnings can be traced back to the Exodus and giving of the Law, nearly 700 years before the fall of Samaria—well in advance, and consistently throughout, those 700 years. Each true prophet—those whose messages are recorded and those who aren't—gave this same warning, a warning that increased during the time immediately preceding the invasion and resulting exile.

The same could be said for the people of Judah, who'd also been amply foretold. Despite warnings, even as the Assyrians closed in on Judah, the people didn't believe God would ever bring judgment. They didn't believe God would ever pull the trigger.

Their attitude is revealed in Ezekiel 12, "Son of man, what is this proverb you have in the land of Israel: 'The days go by and every vision comes to nothing?"' (Ezekiel 12:22, NIV). God tells Ezekiel that He hears and knows the people of Judah say He'll never bring the judgment of which He instructed the prophets to warn. Think how amazing this is. Ezekiel isn't talking about the Assyrian invasion, but rather the Babylonian invasion in 586 B.C. Remember, this was almost one hundred and fifty years after the exile of the ten tribes. By Ezekiel's time, the nation of Israel was gone, and Judah had experienced firsthand the Babylonian exile of its king and some of its people.

You may recall that it hadn't been too long since the Assyrians took forty-six Judean cities and had brought the city of Jerusalem to near defeat. Before that, the nation of Israel in the north experienced the exile of the ten tribes. Backing up even further, there were many times when God allowed a military loss or an attack because of the disobedience of His people. And let's not forget the clear testimony of the flood. Without question, God *does* execute judgment.

Yet, in the time of Ezekiel, God's people generally believed, and even commonly said, that the Lord would never actually do what He said He would do. If this was true at this point in history, certainly it was the case when the Assyrians invaded Israel. When the prophets warned of impending doom, most likely everyone brushed it off. They didn't believe God would let the shoe drop. They didn't believe He'd pull the trigger.

But He did.

He has many times.

He's patient, but He'll take action.

In response to their saying that He'd never do anything, God told Ezekiel to tell the people,

> Say to them, "This is what the Sovereign Lord says: I am going to put an end to this proverb, and they will no longer quote it in Israel." Say to them, "The days are

58

*near when every vision will be fulfilled. For there will be no more false visions or flattering divinations among the people of Israel. But I the Lord will speak what I will, and it shall be fulfilled without delay. For in your days, you rebellious people, I will fulfill whatever I say, declares the Sovereign Lord"* (Ezekiel 12:23-25, NIV).

God did what He told Ezekiel He'd do, and we'll cover that next week. But He also did to Israel what He warned through Moses, Amos, Micah, Isaiah, and others.

# Now

The proverb of the people, mentioned in Ezekiel 12, is much like the popular sentiment in this day and age. It's likely something we'd say. The particular application to that warning is regarding the end of the age, but it stands as truth to all that could happen in life and especially as a consequence of sin. We may not say it as they did in that day, we might say or at least think, "that'll never happen to us."

The Biblical record, history, and our lives would say otherwise.

It can happen to us.

If it's punishment for sin or a promise from God, we can bet He'll pull the trigger.

If it's general difficulty in life, we can also expect that calamities can happen to us. Peter wrote in His epistle a warning of this reality, **"Dear friends, do not be surprised at the fiery ordeal that has come on you to test you, as though something strange were happening to you" (1 Peter 4:12, NIV).**

# INSTRUCTION FOR UNCERTAIN TIMES:
## GOD WILL PULL THE TRIGGER

# 12

## IN UNCERTAIN TIMES
# PRAY

*From Isaiah 30 & 31, 2 Kings 18-19*
*Drawn from the Assyrian attack, siege, and exile of God's people.*

# THEN

Have you ever thought about what it might be like to be king, even for a day? I can't imagine being a king. Well, I *can* imagine the good parts! But the responsibility—no!

I especially cannot imagine the responsibility of protecting an entire nation from the most ruthless fighting force in the world; it's even more difficult to imagine carrying that responsibility after witnessing that army invade and destroy my larger and more powerful neighbors.

No, I don't want any of that part of the king gig.

I mean, the palace, food, wealth, and authority—bring that on. But not so much the responsibility.

King Hezekiah found himself caught in an exceedingly difficult aspect of kingship.

As you read in this week's introduction, Assyria invaded the northern ten tribes [aka Israel] which led to Israel's fall in 722 B.C.

Twenty years later, after not paying the demanded annual tribute, Judah found itself facing the same threat. King Sennacherib marched into Judah, bent on razing her to the ground. He came close, too. Forty-six cities fell.

Hezekiah watched as each city was destroyed, knowing Sennacherib zeroed in with Jerusalem in his sights.

Judah's king defended his people with all his power, but his efforts fell way short. Eventually, every effort he made proved less than good enough—185,000 soldiers surrounded the walls of Jerusalem. Jerusalem's estimated population of only 6,000 produced nowhere near enough soldiers to defend the city.

Attempts to garner support from Egypt or Babylon failed.

Attempts to fortify the city weren't good enough.

Attempts to train and equip an army weren't comprehensive enough.

Attempts to supply the city were good but failed.

Besieged and surrounded, the fate of Israel and the other cities of Judah was soon to be shared by Jerusalem.

To add insult to defeat, the Assyrian king sent Hezekiah a letter. That letter is recorded in 2 Chronicles 32:10-15,

> *"This is what Sennacherib king of Assyria says: On what are you basing your confidence, that you remain in Jerusalem under siege? When Hezekiah says, 'The Lord our God will save us from the hand of the king of Assyria,' he is misleading you, to let you die of hunger and thirst. Did not Hezekiah himself remove this god's high places and altars, saying to Judah and Jerusalem, 'You must worship before one altar and burn sacrifices on it'? "Do you not know what I and my predecessors have done to all the peoples of the other*

*lands? Were the gods of those nations ever able to deliver their land from my hand? Who of all the gods of these nations that my predecessors destroyed has been able to save his people from me? How then can your god deliver you from my hand? Now do not let Hezekiah deceive you and mislead you like this. Do not believe him, for no god of any nation or kingdom has been able to deliver his people from my hand or the hand of my predecessors. How much less will your god deliver you from my hand!" (2 Chronicles 32:10-15).*

Oof. Imagine the weight of this responsibility. I can't. Likely, I'd be like Hezekiah and try to solve my problems in my power, but soon he was out of options.

So, with no other option, King Hezekiah did the one thing he should have done first—He prayed.

I love the image of this prayer in 2 Kings 19:14-19. It's recorded, "Hezekiah received the letter from the messengers and read it. Then he went up to the Temple of the Lord and spread it out before the Lord."

Nothing left to do.

He goes into the presence of God and lays out the letter.

And as we will see, God intervenes—big time!

# NOW

The uncertainty and distress Hezekiah faced was insurmountable; there was nothing he could do in his power to fix the situation. It all was out of his control.

That is the case with national distress. We can't fix it. We can't even begin to fix it. It takes more than us. It impacts more than us.

Even in our personal uncertainties, often they are out of our reach, even if we're trying to fix them.

Yet, we have a God who wants us to take those problems to Him.

He wants us to "spread the letter" out before Him.

He wants us to pray.

He invites us to pray.

He promises answers.

It's likely unfair to assume the event of Hezekiah going into the Temple to pray was the first time he prayed about the situation. I highly doubt it was the first, but I tend to think of it as the first to be that earnest.

After losing forty-six cities, one would think an earnest prayer like that would have come earlier, but from what we read of Isaiah's warning and instruction to him, it seems Hezekiah held out hope one of his measures would work.

Maybe Assyria would change its mind and accept a tribute payment.

Maybe Babylon would swoop in, or maybe Egypt.

Maybe supplies would last.

Hezekiah, though a godly king, seemed reluctant to put the fix-all upon the Lord, but it seems that God wants such a responsibility. That's why we find the Apostle Paul providing instruction like, "**Do not be anxious about anything, but in every situation, by prayer and petition, with thanksgiving, present your requests to God. And the peace of God, which transcends all understanding, will guard your hearts and your minds in Christ Jesus" (Philippians 4:6-7, NIV).**

# INSTRUCTION FOR UNCERTAIN TIMES: PRAY

# 13

## IN UNCERTAIN TIMES
# GOD ANSWERS PRAYER

*From 2 Kings 18-19*
*Drawn from the Assyrian attack, siege, and exile of God's people.*

# THEN

After trying everything in his power to save Jerusalem from the Assyrians, King Hezekiah's back was against the wall. All his efforts were in vain. After receiving a letter from the Assyrian king, Hezekiah took the letter and spread it out in the Temple.

He laid this terrible situation at the feet of the Lord.

He prayed.

It's an opportunity all of God's people have— "to cast our cares upon Him."

We cast our cares upon Him through prayer.

It's not just an opportunity, it's an invitation.

It's a desire of God to hear from His people.

How can we not be amazed that the creator and sustainer of all things, the Sovereign One, God, allows us to petition Him? We may not only petition Him, but He gives us the audacious honor of asking Him to intervene and move on our behalf.

He does. Truly.

Amazing, isn't it?

In the case of King Hezekiah and Judah, the king had no equity from his actions to go to the throne. The default understanding of God's people should be to seek Yahweh first before taking action. He has promised repeatedly to fight for His people. Over and over again He has called on them to turn to and trust Him.

Judah did the opposite.

King Hezekiah did the opposite.

Still, the prayer request was made and heard.

And God answered.

He answered big.

Overnight the Angel of the Lord came and slaughtered all the 185,000 Assyrian soldiers.

The threat was over, just like that.

That's what God can do.

This may be the largest army recorded that God Himself wiped out overnight, but it's far from the only time He executed the impossible.

He answered Hezekiah's prayer. What if Hezekiah had prayed sooner? I'm sure the people of Lachish would have appreciated him doing so. Lachish is the most famous of the forty-six cities destroyed by Sennacherib.

# NOW

As stated in the previous day's devotional, God wants us to ask Him for what we need, and He displays evidence in Scripture of wanting to answer our prayers.

And He does answer prayers.

There's nothing greater we can do for our nation and especially for our own lives than to lay our concerns before God—to pray.

As we learned earlier—God hears. Not only does He hear, but He already knows. More than that, He knows what is ultimately best for us. He also knows what the future holds.

This greater picture, which only God possesses, guides His answer to our prayer. Understand, He always hears, but He doesn't always answer to the degree Hezekiah experienced.

God is always fully capable of destroying an entire army surrounding us, but He doesn't always choose to do so.

He is completely able to calm the waves and wind, but He doesn't always do so. Sometimes something greater needs to be accomplished through the distress before a nation or an individual experiences God's intervention. We don't know what is best, He does, but that should never stop us from laying it out before Him. Whatever the proverbial letter we receive, like Hezekiah, we must lay it out before Him. We need to pray. He will hear. He can do all—even supernaturally blow our minds —with His answer.

We aren't the ones to decide what prayers should be answered or not. We're just asked to pray. We aren't the ones to decide if something is hopeless or not. We're simply asked to pray. And who knows? God may solve everything overnight, or He may not. Regardless, He can do all, and He wants us to ask. Listen to what Jesus said,

**"Ask and it will be given to you; seek and you will find; knock and the door will be opened to you. For everyone who asks receives; the one who seeks finds; and to the one who knocks, the door will be opened" (Matthew 7:7-8, NIV).**

These words, spoken by Jesus and recorded by Matthew, definitely sound like they're given from One who wants to and who will answer prayers. Jesus had been with the Father before His first advent. He knew the desire of the Father and how the Father answers prayers.

Jesus also knew that, for the believers of the future who would pray according to this passage, He'd intercede in prayer. We also know, since Scripture was inspired by the Holy Spirit, that God wants us to know this truth.

So, in uncertain times—pray.

And in uncertain times—God will answer prayers.

He'll answer your prayers.

In Genesis 18, we find Abraham praying that Sodom would be preserved in the coming judgment. That prayer in uncertainty led to the rescue of his nephew Lot.

Pray. God answers.

# INSTRUCTION FOR UNCERTAIN TIMES:
## GOD ANSWERS PRAYERS

# 14
## IN UNCERTAIN TIMES
# TRUST GOD

*From Isaiah 30 & 31, 2 Kings 18-19*
*Drawn from the Assyrian attack, siege, and exile of God's people.*

# THEN

The title today, "In Uncertain Times Trust God," may seem so simple and leave you thinking, "well, duh." You might even be tempted to skip it, but I encourage you not to do that. Trusting God seems to be a no-brainer instruction that God's people understand and automatically follow. Isn't that what all our faith boils down to? Trust?

Trust God.

Sounds easy, doesn't it?

As people of God, we're told to live by faith and trust the Lord.

Paul tells the believers in Rome (and all of us who'd later read his epistle through the ages): "the righteous shall live by faith" (Romans 1:17, NIV).

This was nothing new, but how God always expected His people to live. Paul quoted from the prophet Habakkuk. We also know in Hebrews 11, the chapter often called the "Hall of Faith," we see the most faithful of God's people commended for their faith.

The writer of Hebrews writes:

> *All these people were still living by faith when they died.*
> *They did not receive the things promised; they only saw*
> *them and welcomed them from a distance, admitting*
> *that they were foreigners and strangers on earth. People*
> *who say such things show that they are looking for a*
> *country of their own. If they had been thinking of the*
> *country they had left, they would have had opportunity*
> *to return. Instead, they were longing for a better*
> *country—a heavenly one. Therefore God is not*
> *ashamed to be called their God, for he has prepared a*
> *city for them (Hebrews 11:13-16, NIV).*

Faith, or trusting God, has always been the expectation God has had for His people. It's meant to be our default modus operandi. It's not easy though.

From first calling Israel out of Egypt, God told them to trust Him, that He'd fight for them. He'd give them victory. He'd defeat their enemies.

He also told them not to make any treaty with any other nation, for He'd protect them.

When King Hezekiah came to power in Judah, the Israelites were under the thumb of the bully of the neighborhood, Assyria. They paid a tribute to Assyria, as did other nations.

Babylon, not yet a superpower and smaller than Assyria at this point, reached out to nations asking them to join Babylon in rebellion against the Assyrians. Hezekiah's actions indicate that he bought into this revolt talk, in that he stopped paying their annual tribute, and later in his reign, Hezekiah hosted an envoy from Babylon.

So, it seems Hezekiah led Israel to break from its position as an Assyrian tribute state without seeking the Lord, then reached out to Babylon for defense help. Even more so than pursuing Babylon, Hezekiah courted Egypt.

Isaiah, prophet of Judah during the reign of Hezekiah, was called on to confront the Judean king. The prophet told how God would ultimately give victory over Assyria if Judah would return to Him. "People of Zion, who live in Jerusalem, you will weep no more. How gracious he will be when you cry for help! As soon as he hears, he will answer you" (Isaiah 30:19).

The Lord makes this promised victory clear, "Return, you Israelites, to the One you have so greatly revolted against...' Assyria will fall by no human sword; a sword, not of mortals, will devour them'..." (Isaiah 31:6-8).

Yet, Hezekiah continued to pursue alliances with Babylon and Egypt. This led Isaiah to proclaim boldly:

> *Woe to those who go down to Egypt for help, who rely on horses, who trust in the multitude of their chariots and in the great strength of their horsemen, but do not look to the Holy One of Israel, or seek help from the Lord. Yet he too is wise and can bring disaster; he does not take back his words. He will rise up against that wicked nation, against those who help evildoers. But the Egyptians are mere mortals and not God; their horses are flesh and not spirit. When the Lord stretches out his hand, those who help will stumble, those who are helped will fall; all will perish together (Isaiah 31:1-3).*

Though King Hezekiah is commended as a godly king and

celebrated for the victory God gave during his reign, he was reluctant to simply trust God. His slowness to trust was foolish, definitely after what we read over the last two devotionals. When he finally humbled himself and trusted the Lord—God answered, in a big way.

# Now

My best friend and I spent a lot of time fishing while we were in High School. Throughout our trips, we'd often spend most of the time talking about our *struggles.* It sounds odd, I know, but oh how I'd love to go back and only have to deal with just those struggles. During those trips, we'd spend the whole time catching only a few fish while mostly trying to solve the worlds' problems. Every time the discussion would end the same, coming down to just one thing—trusting God.

Everything came down to faith.

I remember my friend making that point, "Jake, it all comes down to trusting Him."

It sounds so simple.

In Hezekiah's case, God said He'd fight for Israel and defeat the Assyrians, yet it took Hezekiah until the last second to ask and trust God at His Word.

Foolish.

Ridiculous.

Common.

Too close to home.

It's what I do, what about you?

All we need to do is trust Him.

All we need to do is live by faith, as Paul restated from Habakkuk: **"…The righteous will live by faith" (Romans 1:17, NIV).**

# INSTRUCTION FOR UNCERTAIN TIMES:
## TRUST GOD

BABYLONIAN EMPIRE

Week 3

# DISTRESS IN
# BABYLON

# INTRODUCTION
# DISTRESS IN BABYLON

**Uncertain times** again fell upon God's people, the nation of Judah, in the 6th century, with the invasion of King Nebuchadnezzar and the Babylonians. The Babylonians did what the Assyrians almost did to Jerusalem for 120 years—they destroyed the city and the Temple. They also carried many from Judah into captivity in Babylon.

This exile and captivity was the curse that was warned of in the time of Moses, referred to in Deuteronomy. Beginning with Moses and followed by prophet after prophet, the people of Israel were told if they kept the Law and worshipped God they would be blessed and live long in the land, but if they turned from God to idols and sin, they'd be driven from it.

Again and again, the people turned from God. Prophets warned.

Some times of repentance and faithfulness came, but never lasted.

In the 8th century when the Assyrians defeated the Northern Kingdom and nearly took the Southern Kingdom, prophets such as Isaiah and Micah warned that the fate of the Northern Kingdom could be the same for Judah if they didn't repent.

Again, there were flashes of repentance under Hezekiah and later Josiah, but none lasted.

Eventually this led to a couple of sieges and a series of deportations of Jews to Babylon which culminated in the destruction of the city and Temple.

First a group of nobles were taken from Jerusalem and carried to Babylon which included Daniel, Shadrach, Meshach, Abednego.

Next, Jerusalem fell under siege and the king of Judah, Jehoiachin, was exiled. The prophet Ezekiel was believed to be in the group that was taken at this time.

While these conflicts and deportations occurred, the prophet Jeremiah prophesied in Jerusalem that judgment was coming, and Judah needed to repent. At the same time, Ezekiel prophesied to the captives already in Babylon.

There was no repentance.

The city of Jerusalem fell, and the Temple was destroyed by King Nebuchadnezzar and the Babylonians in 587 or 586 BC (there's a debate as to which year).

The city was left in ruin.

The Temple was in ashes.

The precious articles of the Temple were taken to the royal treasury in Babylon.

Many were killed.

Survivors were led to Babylon where they remained in captivity.

Judah found herself in a foreign land.

Times were difficult.

Times were uncertain.

What were God's people to do?

What would God do?

What was learned by God's people in this time stood as lessons for them for ages to come. These lessons still serve us today.

What can we learn to help us stand firm in national distress?

What can we learn of God to help us in times of chaos and difficulty?

# 15
## IN UNCERTAIN TIMES
# GOD WILL BRING HIS WORD TO PASS

*From Jeremiah 11, Ezekiel 12*
*Drawn from the Babylonian invasion, destruction, exile, and captivity*
*God's people faced.*

# THEN

I'm one who often thinks, "*something* like that won't happen ever to me."

Am I the only one? Surely not!

As the saying goes, "When you point one finger, three fingers are pointing back to you." Of course, that's speaking more about judging or hypocrisy, but I believe it applies to the statistics and probabilities that those *somethings* in life we think aren't going to ever happen to us will happen to us. For, if those *somethings* exist, or will happen, then they could happen to us as much as anyone else.

Bad things.

Challenging things.

Catastrophic things.

They all happen.

They happen to people like you and me.

They *can* happen to you and me.

And they likely will—even more so if God says so.

We've already seen on Day 11 that God will pull the trigger. He will. What He says will come to pass. That *something*, which seems impossible and in a faraway future, will be possible and in the present.

In the Day 11 devotional, I referenced Ezekiel 12 where God speaks of a saying in that day—a saying that sounds all too familiar because, when distress strikes and uncertainty continues, it is important to remember.

> *Say to them, "This is what the Sovereign Lord says: I am going to put an end to this proverb, and they will no longer quote it in Israel." Say to them, "The days are near when every vision will be fulfilled. For there will be no more false visions or flattering divinations among the people of Israel. But I the Lord will speak what I will, and it shall be fulfilled without delay. For in your days, you rebellious people, I will fulfill whatever I say, declares the Sovereign Lord"* (Ezekiel 12:23-25, NIV).

Oof. Strong words.

I feel we lack a healthy fear that God will pull the trigger or that His Word will come to pass—that He will do what He says He will do. Judah lacked that fear just 100 years after the ten tribes of the north were carried away at the hands of the Assyrians.

The Israelites received the same warnings of pending exile from their land if idolatry continued, and if they refused to turn back to God. Not only did the people of Judah receive the same warning written in the Law, but prophets were also sent to give them this same warning—sometimes even the same prophets.

Remember, the warnings had been recorded for at least 700 years by the time the Assyrians invaded the north. Prophets relayed the messages consistently throughout that time.

While we may lean toward judging the people of Judah rather harshly for their stubborn disobedience, I almost want to give them a small pass. Think about it. Before the fall of Samaria in 722 BC, they had not seen God come through or "make good" on that long-warned threat. However, I said, "almost." My window of grace for them quickly closes because in 605 BC the Babylonian deportations started, during the fall of Jerusalem, so by 586 BC they were without excuse. Not only were they aware of those warnings, but they also had real evidence before them. If not for the supernatural rescue when God smote the Assyrian army—the same army that besieged Jerusalem—they would have suffered the same fate as those to the north.

At the first sign of another pending siege, the people of Judah would have been wise to repent, but they did not. Amazingly, Jeremiah, who prophesied at that time, said if they would have repented, God would have relented.

That *something* happened to a generation living in Judah.

God did pull the trigger, again.

He did what He said He would.

He brought His Word to pass.

# Now

Our hearts must break.

We must respond to God's warnings.

National distress or trials in our lives may be present because of sin, therefore we must repent. Even if trials or distress in our lives aren't the consequence of sin, uncertain times should call us to repent and seek God—to not only turn back but *run* back to Him.

Distress should bring us to our knees and open our mouths to confess because we, too, have the warning of judgment coming upon our nations and ourselves. Like Judah, we know nations will fall—our nation will one day fall. All nations will be judged. Therefore, the same warning that applied to Judah then still exists and applies to us today. Let us be reminded, God will pull the trigger. Let's check our pride and hard-heartedness. Let's not be like Judah in this matter. Judean grandparents witnessed the destruction of 46 cities and the siege of Jerusalem. They saw what happened to the north, but just two or three generations later, it seemed forgotten.

Maybe not forgotten—maybe met with indifference—but whatever the case, it was costly.

This isn't just a national concept, but it also applies to our own lives. Uncertain times should bring us to personal repentance, or else we will make the same mistake.

God will pull the trigger again.

God will bring His Word to pass.

However, heed this: while we still draw breath into our lungs, the opportunity to repent exists, and repent we should. The instruction given in 1 Chronicles 7:14 is often applied nationally, which to an extent is true. In context, the instruction applies particularly to the Jewish people concerning their nation and their covenant. However, I believe it also should serve as a guiding principle of how we should respond in difficult times. The whole premise behind the passage affirms that God will bring His Word to pass, therefore: **"Humble [yourself] and pray and seek my face and turn from [your] wicked ways, then I will hear from heaven, and I will forgive [your] sin and will heal [your] land [or your life]" (2 Chronicles 7:14, NIV).**

One other note: Since God brings His Word to pass, the good things He promised will also come to pass.

The promised rewards.

The promised Kingdom.

The promised new eternal body.

The promised eternal life.

All of it. Everything He promised will come to pass.

# INSTRUCTION FOR UNCERTAIN TIMES: GOD WILL BRING HIS WORD TO PASS

# 16
## IN UNCERTAIN TIMES
# GOD MAY ALLOW YOU TO SUFFER

*From Jeremiah 12 & 20*
*Drawn from the Babylonian invasion, destruction, exile, and captivity*
*God's people faced.*

# THEN

God may allow you to suffer. Uplifting title, huh?

Did you circle back to the cover to make sure you chose a devotional book?

Truly, this must be the worst title for such a book.

One thing you probably already noticed—although this devotional book is for *such a time as this* and was written to provide biblical truth to help us in these times—not every devotional feels encouraging. However, as God's people, encouragement can always be found in the hope—even if just a thread—within all things.

The mix of sobering truths, challenging instruction, and encouragement in this devotional book reflects exactly what we're committed to sharing—relaying the truth. Stand Firm Books promises no FLUFF!

In all fairness, seeing today's title, "God May Allow You to Suffer" generates everything opposite to "warm fuzzies." It's strange to write this for the USA in this day and age, ordinarily, but so much now is anything but ordinary for the USA.

Transparently, I've struggled in writing this—asking, "Lord, is this really what I need to write?" Many marketers would likely blow a gasket at this endeavor—hence the need for Stand Firm Books. Truth trumps feelings because truth matters more.

The Biblical truth for God's care in uncertain times just happens to be what we're sharing now. Scripture talks about judgment, repentance, our need to rise up, *and* encouragement.

There is something Christians throughout most of Christian history—and those in various parts of the world right now—grasp that we don't. As believers in the USA, we cannot fathom the reasons why we may incur suffering. We may suffer due to our beliefs, or even because of our righteousness. Even in such trials, God still loves us. He's still good. He's still all-powerful, and He still cares. Along with that seeming paradox, we're to remain encouraged amid those trials.

God allows suffering.

In the time of the Babylonian invasion and destruction of Jerusalem, God called Jeremiah to be a prophet, to explain what was happening and give one last call for the people to repent.

The task of a prophet was never easy, but the context in which Jeremiah preached was more difficult than most all of the prophets. Yet, he still obeyed. Jeremiah lived faithfully and carried out this call in a nation turned so far from God that He was sending judgment upon them. This means many, probably seemingly all, were not living for God. Yet even though one of the few righteous and obedient, Jeremiah suffered. He suffered greatly.

Jeremiah's sufferings can be seen in what is called the six Laments of Jeremiah, found in the book of Jeremiah. Here's one of such laments.

> *O LORD, you have enticed me,…*
> *you have overpowered me….*
> *If I say, "I will not mention him [the LORD],*
> *or speak any more in his name,"*
> *then within me there is something like a burning fire*
> *shut up in my bones;*
> *I am weary with holding it in,*
> *and I cannot….*
> *Why did I come forth from the womb*
> *to see toil and sorrow,*
> *and spend my days in shame?* (Jeremiah 20:7a, 9, 18).

During his time as prophet, Jeremiah saw little to no fruit. He faced criticism and ostracism from fellow countrymen. Jeremiah endured the dreadful Babylonian siege of Jerusalem. He dealt with heartache for his fellow Judeans. At one point, he was imprisoned, later kidnapped, and taken to Egypt. Tradition holds that he was stoned to death by his fellow Judeans, who grew sick of his call for repentance.

# Now

Jeremiah suffered, as did nearly every other prophet.

Speaking of the suffering these prophets faced, their faith is recognized in Hebrews 11:37-38:

> *They were put to death by stoning; they were sawed in two; they were killed by the sword. They went about in sheepskins and goatskins, destitute, persecuted and mistreated—the world was not worthy of them. They wandered in deserts and mountains, living in caves and in holes in the ground* (Hebrews 11:37-38).

Suffering didn't stop in the Old Testament.

Jesus suffered. He was crucified.

The disciples suffered.

Believers throughout the ages have suffered.

Believers today suffer.

God allows suffering.

So, when difficulty comes on a nation or in your life—know it's normal for the faithful people of God. God hasn't fallen off His throne. He hasn't stopped caring.

How normal can suffering be for the faithful believer? Listen to Jesus' own words, "Remember the word that I said to you: 'A servant is not greater than his master.' If they persecuted me, they will also persecute you. If they kept my word, they will also keep yours" (John 15:20).

Though suffering is normal, motivation to endure is echoed in Hebrews 11, **"Instead, they were longing for a better country—a heavenly one. Therefore, God is not ashamed to be called their God, for he has prepared a city for them" (Hebrews 11:16, NIV).**

# INSTRUCTION FOR UNCERTAIN TIMES:
## GOD MAY ALLOW SUFFERING

# 17

## IN UNCERTAIN TIMES
# TRUST IN GOD'S WORD

*From Daniel 1*
*Drawn from the Babylonian invasion, destruction, exile, and captivity*
*God's people faced.*

# THEN

Daniel, the famed survivor of the lion's den (to be addressed later), was a contemporary of Jeremiah—younger, but still a contemporary. A young boy in the time Jeremiah prophesied, Daniel was deported to Babylon in the first wave of exile. He was a son of nobility and the Babylonians practiced the routine of bringing the young ruling class of the nations they captured into the court of King Nebuchadnezzar.

Three others are named to have been taken in that same group—Hananiah, Mishael, and Azariah, known best by their Babylonian names: Shadrach, Meshach, and Abednego. They are the famed survivors of the fiery furnace.

Before the lion's den and the fiery furnace, these four young men were brought into the king's court and offered food and wine from Nebuchadnezzar's table—the best selection of food in the world at the time. Oh, the allure to eat like kings and not just any king, but kings of the world's most powerful empire.

I'm already tempted to try this grub—you?

This past year I committed to becoming healthier. On this health journey process, I've discovered a lot of my tendencies toward food. If I become frustrated, or something doesn't work out like I think it should, then making healthy decisions go out the window. I give up elsewhere in life, especially in eating right.

Ever heard of stress eating? Yep, that's one of my habits, too. When I'm stressed, I munch, munch, munch.

You may relate.

I share that because if I was one of these four young men, I might become frustrated with life and be tempted to toss all the things I ever tried to do right—just give up.

Daniel had good reason to be frustrated. He was uprooted from his home and family and held captive in a foreign land. No doubt he endured great hardship in the process of becoming exiled. On top of his struggle, his home nation was being destroyed, his family and the people he loved killed.

He had the right to give up on the righteous acts he kept.

He had the right to give up on his faith.

Yet, when offered the amazing bounty of the king's table, he asked permission to eat only vegetables and water.

We think in terms of Daniel wanting to be on a specific diet—the Daniel Plan—but Daniel wasn't being health-conscious; he was being faithful to God. The word in English used to describe his reasoning for his choice was "defile." He didn't want to defile himself, meaning he didn't want to break the Mosaic Law he faithfully kept by eating things forbidden.

Pork and chevaline (horse meat) were staples in Babylon and forbidden in the Law. Also, the food and drink more likely had been part of pagan sacrificial rituals.

The key to Daniel maintaining his faith, even in this seemingly small detail shows, even into the most uncertain of times, he kept the Law.

He held on to his faith.

He trusted the promises of God.

He trusted God's Word.

# NOW

At Daniel's young age, and in those dire circumstances, I'm amazed he kept the dietary laws. However, he trusted God's way as best. Daniel also maintained that same trust even as God allowed calamity in his life and his nation. He trusted God's Word as truth.

The rightness of God's Word is not contingent on immediate circumstances. His truth stands through time. Even when the proverbial rug is pulled out from under us, we must continue to not only trust God but to trust in His Word—in the Scriptures.

We cannot let circumstances change the Word, rather the Word should change our circumstances, or at least our attitude in those circumstances.

God gave His Word knowing all that would happen in the nations in which we live, and all that would happen in our lives. He knows the big picture.

Even if we feel abandoned by God, confused or frustrated that He allowed some great disaster to fall upon us, we must not throw out the rest of the Word.

A friend who lost her husband and children in a car accident answered a common question asked by her friend after the wreck. The friend asked if she'd still believe in God. My friend replied, "Yes, because if I let go of God, then I lose the chance to see my family again."

Though calamity came she still clung to God's promises in His Word. God declared through the prophet Isaiah that God's Word would stand and accomplish God's purpose, **"so is my word that goes out from my mouth. It will not return to me empty, but will accomplish what I desire and achieve the purpose for which I sent it" (Isaiah 55:11, NIV).**

## INSTRUCTION FOR UNCERTAIN TIMES:
### TRUST GOD'S WORD

# 18
## IN UNCERTAIN TIMES
# BET ON GOD

*From Daniel 2*
*Drawn from the Babylonian invasion, destruction, exile, and captivity*
*God's people faced.*

# THEN

My wife refuses to ever let me set foot inside a casino, not that I would, but that's beside the point.

She feels this way for multiple reasons, but for one she knows I never know when to stop—I don't. I'm the guy who dropped a whole roll of quarters in one of those stuffed animal crane machines. I kept trying because I just knew the next drop of the crane would be the *one*—the stuffed animal payday.

Though I possess all the signs of what might likely be a dangerous gambler, I refrain from betting—eh, mostly anyway. I lost five dollars to my daughter the other day betting on how a television show would end, so maybe I still do a little betting, but not much.

While serving in King Nebuchadnezzar's court, Daniel made an audacious bet. He bet on God.

He knew God was a sure bet, but the odds were extreme and the wager was huge.

For a little background, the king placed the advisors in his court in an impossible situation. Following a profound and disturbing dream, the king demanded they not only interpret the dream but also tell the dream.

They all failed.

Telling the dream was impossible.

Because of the subjective nature of interpreting dreams, his advisors typically offered smokescreen-type answers, but to tell the contents of the actual dream—now that was tough, crazy even. In Daniel 2:10, those in the court are recorded saying, "There is not a man on earth who can do what the mighty king asks! No king, however great and mighty, has ever asked such a thing."

On top of making this difficult request, King Nebuchadnezzar threatened to kill everyone in his court.

Daniel found himself in a trying situation.

He was going to be killed.

His friends were going to be killed. And others of the court Daniel became acquainted with also faced impending death.

Facing the logical impossibility of telling the content of the king's dream, Daniel bet on God. He knew nothing is impossible for God. Daniel likely never interpreted a dream before this, and even if he had, he certainly never been required to independently discover the content of a dream. Knowing God is fully capable of the impossible, Daniel bet on God.

He asked the king for more time.

The Scriptures say Daniel then found Hananiah, Mishael, and Azariah, and asked them to plead with God to provide an answer. The four men used one of the truths for uncertain times we have already mentioned—they prayed.

God also carried out one of the truths we've mentioned—He answered.

In the night, God gave Daniel the dream and the interpretation. Daniel then told the king and all those in the court were spared. God had been a safe bet.

# Now

The betting line on God and the impossible remains the same since the day of Daniel. God is still a safe bet. He can still do the impossible.

In uncertain times, we need to bet on God in two ways.

First, when we become a follower of Christ, we're making a bet on God, or we could say investing in Him with everything in our lives. Simply put, a Christ-follower bets by trusting that the best payoff is to belong to Jesus and follow Him. Each moment we live we wager our life and eternity on God, or ourselves and this world, so we need to remember God is the winning hand. We will not lose, and ultimately we will gain the whole world by continuing to cling to Him. As others turn away and the world around you scoffs, don't change your bet.

Don't flinch.

Don't fold.

God wins.

If you belong to Him, you have the winning hand, even if it seems the deck is stacked against you.

God holds the ace, the royal flush, the unbeatable hand.

He will win.

Keep on keeping on.

Second, when your back is against the wall in uncertain times, bet on God.

Logically, humanly, there was no possible answer available to Daniel, but he knew God could come through. We must burn that into our minds and keep it in the on-deck circle. When there's no solution or a way to go—bet on God.

He has delivered the impossible over and over again.

He's always able to deliver the impossible, as Jesus once told the disciples, "**Jesus replied, 'What is impossible with man is possible with God'**" (Luke 18:27, NIV).

# INSTRUCTION FOR UNCERTAIN TIMES:
## BET ON GOD

# 19

## IN UNCERTAIN TIMES
# BE WILLING TO BURN

*From Daniel 3*
*Drawn from the Babylonian invasion, destruction, exile, and captivity*
*God's people faced.*

# THEN

After Daniel went "all in" with God regarding King Nebuchadnezzar's dream and the interpretation of it, and after God showed His hand in providing the answers Daniel needed, not only was Daniel's life spared, the lives of his Judean brothers in the court, and the rest of the advisors were spared as well. That's not all. Daniel was promoted to a high position. This promotion positioned him to request his fellow countrymen, Hananiah, Mishael, and Azariah—better known by their Babylonian names as Shadrach, Meshach, and Abednego—to be promoted to govern the province of Babylon.

The dream of the statue must have triggered an idea for the king as he had a gold statue built in his likeness. It stood 90 ft. high and 9 ft. wide. At the statue's completion, the administrators of his empire were gathered to dedicate the statue and ordered to bow before it. All did except for three—Shadrach, Meshach, and Abednego.

99

Seeing this action, Babylonian officials pressured King Nebuchadnezzar to decree that those who refused to bow to the statue be thrown into the large furnace. The three faithful men remained steadfast despite this threat. They refused to bow to other gods or idols. Just as from the beginning of their captivity, Shadrach, Meshach, and Abednego held to God's Word.

In this moment of distress from an oppressive government leader, they practiced some of the truths we've already mentioned.

They stuck to their guns.

They were brave.

They trusted God.

They knew He'd bring His Word to pass.

They trusted in God's Word.

Not only that, but they undoubtedly were willing to burn.

Also, I believe there was certainly crying out to God and praying—I think anyone, believer or not, would be praying as they faced their fate inside a furnace. I also believe Daniel interceded in prayer for them. Oddly, Daniel's not mentioned in this event, but he was likely around. In chapter 2 of The Book of Daniel, it is clear Daniel was retained in the royal court, while the three other Judeans were brought into provincial government. Then in chapter 3, only the provincial administrators are listed. Daniel may have not been bound to bow but was likely there. Knowing what Scripture reveals of Daniel, he was certainly praying.

God heard.

God answered.

Shadrach, Meshach, and Abednego's actions infuriated the king. When they were brought before the king and questioned, the answer they gave was:

*"King Nebuchadnezzar, we do not need to defend ourselves before you in this matter. If we are thrown into the blazing furnace, the God we serve is able to deliver us from it, and he will deliver us from Your Majesty's hand. But even if he does not, we want you to know, Your Majesty, that we will not serve your gods or worship the image of gold you have set up"* (Daniel 3:16-18, NIV).

Their answer didn't help their cause with the king, not that they were worried about him. The king's anger only escalated, and he commanded the fire to be heated seven times hotter. The furnace burned so intensely the flames of the fire killed the soldiers who bound the three, and Shadrach, Meshach, and Abednego fell into the burning flames.

The soldiers died, but not Shadrach, Meshach, and Abednego.

They were seen walking free in the fire, free of their bindings.

Not only that, a fourth person was also seen in the fire with them—the Lord.

The three exited the fire unharmed, not a hair singed, no harm to their clothes, and not even smelling of smoke.

This led to the king then proclaiming the greatness of their God.

# NOW

Shadrach, Meshach, and Abednego stood strong, willing to burn.

As followers of Christ, we're to be willing to do so also.

We may not leave the fire, firing squad, or whatever we face unharmed, but there will be "another in the fire" with us.

The three Hebrew amigos aren't the only ones saved from fires in history.

John the Apostle was thrown into a vat of boiling oil and emerged unharmed. His disciple, Polycarp, was placed at a stake to be burned, but the fire did not touch his body. A dagger thrust into his side caused his demise.

God has miraculously saved His people many, many times, but there have been far more martyrs than those rescued—still, we can be sure there was *another* with all of them, as Jesus promised His disciples then and promises us today, **"Surely I am with you always, to the very end of the age" (Matthew 28:20, NIV).**

# INSTRUCTION FOR UNCERTAIN TIMES:
## BE WILLING TO BURN

## 20

IN UNCERTAIN TIMES
# BE OBEDIENT

*From Ezekiel 2 - 5*
*Drawn from the Babylonian invasion, destruction, exile, and captivity*
*God's people faced.*

# THEN

We began this week discussing Jeremiah who prophesied in Jerusalem immediately before the Babylonian invasion. He preached through the early deportations and up to the destruction of the city. Two other major prophets were in the city with Jeremiah—Daniel and Ezekiel. We've looked at part of Daniel's life already.

Though they were in Jerusalem together, Daniel and Ezekiel would prophesy in Babylon. The two were both exiled. Daniel was taken into the royal court and Ezekiel lived beside the Kebar River in a settlement of exiled Jewish people. The three were contemporaries.

Jeremiah gave his warnings in Jerusalem. He gave the last warnings of the coming destruction of the city.

Daniel worked within the governments of Babylon and later the Persian empire. Most of his prophecies dealt with the succession of Middle Eastern empires from Babylon and beyond.

Ezekiel was sent among the exiled Jews, calling them to repentance and explaining what was taking place.

These three men, along with all the other prophets throughout the history recorded in the Old Testament, had to follow God with obedience. Imagine the difficulties they faced. God gave them messages contrary to the ideas of society at that time and they were not well received. Yet, they spoke on behalf of Him no matter the cost—even being willing to pay with their lives.

Now, obedience isn't reserved only for the prophets. All God's people are meant to obey His commands. Though we're all called to obedience, the Book of Ezekiel gives insight into the importance of our obedience, especially in trying times. The times demanded Ezekiel be completely obedient.

Repeatedly in his calling to be a prophet, as recorded in chapters 1 and 2 of Ezekiel, it is stated that he must obey—he must say and do exactly what God tells him to do. Listen to this charge given to the prophet in Ezekiel 2:8: "But you, son of man, listen to what I say to you. Do not rebel like that rebellious people."

Not only was he warned not to rebel, but his obedience was critically important because the repentance of the nation hinged on the message he brought. The vitalness of his obedience is made even more evident in Ezekiel 3:

> "Son of man, I have made you a watchman for the people of Israel; so hear the word I speak and give them warning from me. When I say to a wicked person, 'You will surely die,' and you do not warn them or speak out to dissuade them from their evil ways in order to save their life, that wicked person will die for their sin, and I will hold you accountable for their blood. But if you do warn the wicked person and they do not turn from their

*wickedness or from their evil ways, they will die for their sin; but you will have saved yourself. "Again, when a righteous person turns from their righteousness and does evil, and I put a stumbling block before them, they will die. Since you did not warn them, they will die for their sin. The righteous things that person did will not be remembered, and I will hold you accountable for their blood. But if you do warn the righteous person not to sin and they do not sin, they will surely live because they took warning, and you will have saved yourself" (Ezekiel 3:17-21, NIV).*

If Ezekiel failed to obey, the blood of the people would be on his hands.

Ezekiel's role in those uncertain times was vital. God allowed Judah to be invaded and Jerusalem destroyed. He allowed His own people to be taken into captivity—not out of spite, but as discipline. Ezekiel was sent to explain the disciplinary actions of God and to instruct the people on how they should respond. He also brought hope to them in very trying times.

Throughout the whole Book of Ezekiel, we see God call Ezekiel to do crazy things and the times demanded the prophet to obey.

Ezekiel did all that he was told to do.

He was obedient to God.

# NOW

It may be easy for us to see all that depended upon Ezekiel's obedience to God—doing and saying all he was instructed to do and say—but in the midst of his work, Ezekiel probably didn't see things quite so clearly.

Have you ever looked out an airplane window and viewed the land from an aerial perspective? I'm always amazed. From above, there seem to be all these perfect squares and it looks all neat and organized, but on the ground, in the midst of it all, it can seem like a mess.

I imagine this is a good analogy for how Ezekiel saw things.

He had been taken from his home.

He was now living in a refugee camp.

He was in captivity.

There was much uncertainty.

Everything familiar to Ezekiel had been uprooted.

While trying to navigate through his personal upheaval, and still facing national trials along with others from Judah, God called Ezekiel to preach this difficult message.

Yet, he was obedient.

The people of Judah needed him to be obedient.

We may or may not be given the monumental task of speaking on behalf of God in great trials like those Ezekiel faced. The magnitude of the task(s) God gives us isn't what matters. The sobering fact is that repentance and the faithfulness of others to follow Christ hinge on our obedience.

Oof. That's serious stuff.

Obedience to God is always important, but even more so when daily life and the times we face become increasingly difficult.

Therefore, in uncertain times we must not merely seek God to hear from Him, but we must completely obey, **"Since we live by the Spirit, let us keep in step with the Spirit" (Galatians 5:25, NIV).**

# INSTRUCTION FOR UNCERTAIN TIMES:
## BE OBEDIENT

# 21
## IN UNCERTAIN TIMES
# BE BOLD

*From Ezekiel 2 – 6, 12 - 13*
*Drawn from the Babylonian invasion, destruction, exile, and captivity*
*God's people faced.*

# THEN

Though evidence seems to show there weren't many who accepted it, the exiled people of Judah needed Ezekiel's message. The godly instruction and encouragement were vital for them to repent and turn back to God in order to see the end of captivity and the restoration of the nation.

As mentioned in Day 20, Ezekiel received a tall order from God and obedience was crucial. However, obedience wasn't all that the message demanded; instruction and encouragement needed to be delivered with boldness.

In such a crisis, Ezekiel could not be timid but rather had to preach with boldness.

Time was too short.

Too much was at stake.

He delivered a message contrary to the entire society and placed himself at odds against almost every other so-called prophet.

"Son of man, prophesy against the prophets of Israel who are now prophesying. Say to those who prophesy out of their own imagination: 'Hear the word of the Lord! This is what the Sovereign Lord says: Woe to the foolish prophets who follow their own spirit and have seen nothing! Your prophets, Israel, are like jackals among ruins. You have not gone up to the breaches in the wall to repair it for the people of Israel so that it will stand firm in the battle on the day of the Lord. Their visions are false and their divinations a lie. Even though the Lord has not sent them, they say, "The Lord declares," and expect him to fulfill their words. Have you not seen false visions and uttered lying divinations when you say, "The Lord declares," though I have not spoken? "'Therefore, this is what the Sovereign Lord says: Because of your false words and lying visions, I am against you, declares the Sovereign Lord. My hand will be against the prophets who see false visions and utter lying divinations. They will not belong to the council of my people or be listed in the records of Israel, nor will they enter the land of Israel. Then you will know that I am the Sovereign Lord. "'Because they lead my people astray, saying, "Peace," when there is no peace, and because, when a flimsy wall is built, they cover it with whitewash, therefore tell those who cover it with whitewash that it is going to fall. Rain will come in torrents, and I will send hailstones hurtling down, and violent winds will burst forth. When the wall collapses, will people not ask you, "Where is the whitewash you covered it with?"* (Ezekiel 13:2-12).

He delivered a message difficult for the people to hear. Though true, it exposed their sin and contrasted their view of God.

"Son of man, set your face against the mountains of Israel; prophesy against them and say: 'You mountains of Israel, hear the word of the Sovereign Lord. This is what the Sovereign Lord says to the mountains and hills, to the ravines and valleys: I am about to bring a sword against you, and I will destroy your high places. Your altars will be demolished, and your incense altars will be smashed; and I will slay your people in front of your idols. I will lay the dead bodies of the Israelites in front of their idols, and I will scatter your bones around your altars. Wherever you live, the towns will be laid waste and the high places demolished, so that your altars will be laid waste and devastated, your idols smashed and ruined, your incense altars broken down, and what you have made wiped out. Your people will fall slain among you, and you will know that I am the Lord. "But I will spare some, for some of you will escape the sword when you are scattered among the lands and nations. Then in the nations where they have been carried captive, those who escape will remember me—how I have been grieved by their adulterous hearts, which have turned away from me, and by their eyes, which have lusted after their idols. They will loathe themselves for the evil they have done and for all their detestable practices. And they will know that I am the Lord; I did not threaten in vain to bring this calamity on them. "This is what the Sovereign Lord says: Strike your hands together and

109

*stamp your feet and cry out "Alas!" because of all the wicked and detestable practices of the people of Israel, for they will fall by the sword, famine, and plague. One who is far away will die of the plague, and one who is near will fall by the sword, and anyone who survives and is spared will die of famine. So, will I pour out my wrath on them* (Ezekiel 13:2-12).

Ezekiel's messages didn't make him popular by any means. Quite the opposite, as I'm sure you can imagine. These are only two excerpts from the many dire warnings the prophet conveyed. Ezekiel's preaching and prophesying weren't the only areas requiring his boldness. As if the messages given weren't difficult enough, God called Ezekiel to do crazy things to speak these truths to the people of Israel. One of these instances is told in Ezekiel 4. Ezekiel lay on his left side in public for 390 days to represent the years of the nation's sin. Then he lay on his right side for 40 days to represent the siege of Jerusalem, and while doing so, he was to cook his food using cow manure to show how the food supply would be cut off from the nation.

This was only one of the many crazy things Ezekiel was instructed to do—and he did them all!

God told Ezekiel that He was making him a sign unto himself. The prophet's ministry wasn't just to speak prophetically, rather the obedience of his life was to display prophecy as well.

# NOW

We may not be given a prophetic calling like Ezekiel, but as believers we've been given the truth. We're given the truth in Scripture—we know what is to come in the future and why. We also have the Holy Spirit indwelling us, and John 16:13 teaches that He will guide us into all the things yet to come. Each of us bears the truth or at least can know the truth amid uncertain times. Today, just as in the time of Ezekiel, sharing that message is crucial. Our loved ones and those in our sphere of influence need the times deciphered and the truth shared. Proclaiming this vital message requires more than a mere whisper of the truth, but a bold proclamation. Whether God gives us a message to share or an action to do, we must be bold.

As for Ezekiel, time is too short, and too much is at stake.

Therefore, in uncertain times we must follow the instruction the Apostle Paul gave Timothy, **"For the Spirit God gave us does not make us timid, but gives us power, love and self-discipline" (2 Timothy 1:7, NIV).**

# INSTRUCTION FOR UNCERTAIN TIMES: BE BOLD

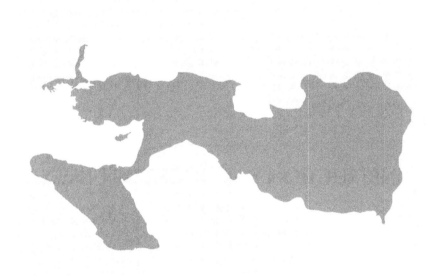

# DISTRESS IN
# PERSIA

Week 4
# INTRODUCTION
# DISTRESS IN PERSIA

**Uncertain times** continued for God's people in the nation of Judah, beginning in 539 BC, when the Babylonian empire in which they were living was captured by the Medes and Persians. For the most part, the exchange of power from Babylon to Persia was a blessing for Judah. It brought the promised reprieve that set Judah free and allowed the people the opportunity to return home. Though life under Persian rule was an improvement, there were times of great challenges including one of the most terrifying moments in Jewish history. Their existence hung in the balance and hinged on the brave actions of one Jewish woman.

Literally overnight, the Persian king, Cyrus, captured the city of Babylon and the empire of the Medes and Persians rose to become the dominating power in the world. Along with acquiring the city and empire from Babylon, Persia gained Babylon's captives, which included Judah. Jews found themselves in the middle of culture and government change once again. As mentioned, for the most part this change was positive, for King Cyrus decreed they could return home, but once again they were under the hand of a foreign ruler.

Though mostly positive, living under any pagan rule had its challenges for the uniquely monotheistic Jewish people. The same temptation of bowing to foreign gods and forsaking their own commands from God remained before them. It would've been hard keeping their unique identity as a nation through trial, punishment, and exile. Scripture gives accounts of some of the challenges faithful Jews like Daniel, Nehemiah, Mordecai, Esther, and others, faced.

Also, during the Persian period, the saga of Israel "went split screen" as some returned to the homeland and the majority continued living on the foreign soul.

In this time period, the Jewish people faced the greatest threat they've ever faced. They had weathered times of national distress, loss of freedom, had their entire way of life and homeland threatened, but in this threat, their existence was on the line. Fortunately, God's providence had already prepared a rescue.

Once again, throughout living under this foreign rule, times were difficult and uncertain.

What were God's people to do?

What would God do?

Lessons learned by God's people in this time stood and served them for ages to come. These lessons still serve us today.

What can we learn to help us stand firm in national distress?

What can we learn of God to help us in times of chaos and difficulty?

# 22

# GOD WILL SEND SIGNS

*From 2 Kings 24 & 25, 2 Chronicles 36, Daniel 5*
*Drawn from when God's people were subject to the Persians.*

## THEN

The life of the prophet Daniel spanned the entire Babylonian captivity, where he served in the Babylonian royal administration. He lived under the Persians also, and he continued to serve in government. From a front-row seat, He witnessed the Persian capture of Babylon.

In the final years of the Babylonian Empire, Babylonian King Nabonidus left. In essence, he took a ten-year vacation. Imagine how that would go over today when our media rips on presidents who spend time golfing. The citizens of Babylon didn't appreciate their absent king, which eventually led many to defect. The king's son, Belshazzar, ruled in his absence as co-regent.

Belshazzar hosted a large banquet, during which he gave instructions for the gold and silver goblets from the Temple in Jerusalem to be brought out for the celebration. These goblets were taken from the Temple when the city and Temple were destroyed by King Nebuchadnezzar. As they drank from these holy cups and praised their

117

gods, a human hand appeared amid their revelry and wrote on the wall. Belshazzar saw this and became extremely frightened. Perhaps "freaked out" would be more accurate given his reaction. His face turned pale, his knees knocked, and his legs gave out. Yeah, he freaked out, wouldn't you?

Following the template of Nebuchadnezzar's disturbing dream, the acting king called together all the wise men in the empire, promising them the position of third in command if they could determine the meaning. No one could.

Who do you think they called?

Yep, cue in Daniel to the rescue.

The Babylonian queen remembered Daniel had once interpreted the dream for King Nebuchadnezzar, so Daniel was summoned and, sure enough, he interpreted the writing.

On the wall, the hand had written, "Mene, mene, tekel, parsin."

Led by the Spirit of God, Daniel revealed the meaning: "Mene: God has numbered the days of your reign and brought it to an end. Tekel: you have been weighed on the scales and found wanting. Peres (parsin): your kingdom is divided and given to the Medes and Persians" (Daniel 5:26-28).

Again, Daniel was correct.

That night the Medes and Persians overtook the city and killed Belshazzar.

This supernatural warning left little time for the Babylonians to alter course. It likely came just a few hours ahead of the destruction. However, whenever oppression came down to God's people, He sent sure signs *something* was coming.

As presented many times in this book, prophets were sent by God to warn His people.

Prophetic messages weren't the only warnings. There were signs of what was coming all around, if only God's people had recognized them.

Though history doesn't tell us, it would seem that before Pharaoh enslaved the Hebrews, there'd be evidence of growing tensions. Perhaps discerning Israelites could have remembered the word passed down from Abraham—their time in Egypt was only a pit stop. They could have also recognized the tension and began "checking their ticket," as we addressed in the first devotion. Tension and seeming evidence of prophetic fulfillment should have caused them to ask questions.

Signs may have been hard to decipher for Israel during their time in Egypt, but clear signs of the Assyrian invasion and Babylonian invasions left them without excuse.

For Judah, the Babylonian exiles and siege happened over a twenty-five-year span. I believe even after the first waves of captives were led to Babylon; Judah could have repented. Maybe they even could have repented during the siege; they should have taken Hezekiah's path of praying.

It's clear that in each of the scenarios where God's people faced national distress, signs were provided in advance.

# NOW

God is still in the business of sending signs ahead of coming challenges. I would argue for modern American believers that the issue isn't seeing the signs, but rather that we're largely missing the internal mental and spiritual database in which the signs trigger alarms for us. We see and bemoan the signs of greater challenges coming, but we don't have the proper awareness of what is happening.

This was likely the case in the past. God's people would have seen tensions building, the decline of their nation, and the rise of another, but they didn't recognize any of this as what it truly was. They were also without excuse because they had the Law and the prophets.

Jesus called his disciples then and calls us today to be aware of the signs happening around us, "**Now learn this lesson from the fig tree: As soon as its twigs get tender and its leaves come out, you know that summer is near. Even so, when you see all these things, you know that it is near, right at the door. Truly I tell you, this generation will certainly not pass away until all these things have happened**" (Matthew 24:32-24, NIV).

# INSTRUCTION FOR UNCERTAIN TIMES: GOD WILL SEND SIGNS

# 23

# GOD WILL GIVE REPRIEVES

*From Daniel 5, 2 Chronicles 36, Ezra 1*
*Drawn from when God's people were subject to the Persians.*

## THEN

When King Cyrus defeated the Babylonians and rode into the city, he saw himself as a liberator. He did liberate the exiled Jews. Amazingly, it happened exactly as the prophet Jeremiah said it would, some fifty to seventy years earlier. Being even more precise, the prophet Isaiah mentioned King Cyrus by name twice—nearly two hundred years before the event happened.

After inheriting the exiled people of God, King Cyrus issued a decree for the Temple to be rebuilt and allowed the Jews to return home.

A reprieve had come.

The captivity had ended.

Jews returned home on a mission to rebuild the Temple.

Conditions for the Jewish people also seemed to ease initially under Persian rule.

Reprieves are constant when there is calamity in the Bible. When God's people face hardship, even the warnings of difficulty always come with a promise that the hardship will end, and better times lie ahead.

There's always hope.

Jeremiah, Ezekiel, and Daniel were the chief prophets of the exile. Jeremiah and Ezekiel especially told of the punishment that had befallen Judah. They pronounced the severity of the city's destruction and captivity. The two didn't mince words about the anger of God due to the people's sin. Yet, in the writings of both, they tell of the end of the captivity. They tell of the people's return and ultimately the establishment of an eternal kingdom. Both even point to the New Covenant.

Daniel speaks a lot about this eternal kingdom to be ruled by the Messiah.

What Cyrus did for the Jewish people was remarkable.

He returned the articles of the Temple taken by Nebuchadnezzar.

He also funded the program to rebuild the Temple.

# NOW

By now we know what God promises, and we know that what He's placed in His Word will come to pass. One devotion you read gave the instruction: God will bring His Word to pass. Another devotion gave the truth: God will pull the trigger. Those truths resurface every time promised calamity comes, but these truths apply to more than just the punishment God will bring to pass or pull the trigger on. He will also bring blessings to pass. Good promises will come true. God will do good things.

He's going to bring punishment.

He's going to allow suffering, but He will also do good. He will bring reprieves.

God's people experience darkness, as we've presented, but there will always be a sunrise.

Though God's people were enslaved in Egypt, they were rescued and brought to the Promised Land.

Though Assyria invaded and destroyed much of the nation, God supernaturally rescued His people.

Though His people received what they deserved for turning from Him and toward idols, the captivity only lasted seventy years.

Though there will always be darkness to walk through, the sun will rise.

Interestingly, in Revelation 22, as the apostle John relays the nature of the New Heavens and New Earth, he writes, "There will be no more night. They will not need the light of a lamp or the light of the sun, for the Lord God will give them light. And they will reign forever and ever" (Revelation 22:4). Therefore, for the believer, dire situations will never end in darkness. Ultimately, darkness will no longer exist, for God the Father will dwell with us.

We can count on these reprieves because it's in God's nature. In Exodus 34, God reveals Himself to Moses more intimately than He has with anyone in history. It was an emphasized moment. What God revealed of Himself at that moment is something we should take to heart. God revealed His nature. Although He'll punish sin, He prefers to give His people mercy and love. **"Then the Lord came down in the cloud and stood there with him and proclaimed his name, the Lord. And he passed in front of Moses, proclaiming, 'The Lord, the Lord, the compassionate and gracious God, slow to anger, abounding in love and faithfulness, maintaining love to thousands, and forgiving wickedness, rebellion and sin. Yet he does not leave the guilty unpunished; he punishes the children** and their children for the sin of the parents to the third and fourth generation'" (Exodus 34:5-7, NIV).

# INSTRUCTION FOR UNCERTAIN TIMES:
## GOD WILL SEND A REPRIEVE

## 24

IN UNCERTAIN TIMES
# KEEP THE VISION

*From Ezra 1 & 2*
*Drawn from when God's people were subject to the Persians.*

## THEN

Following Cyrus' decree, only a small remnant of the Jewish people returned to Jerusalem.

Ezra writes, "…everyone whose heart God had moved— prepared to go up and build the house of the Lord in Jerusalem" (Ezra 1:5, NIV).

This is an interesting statement, we'll come back to examine it.

Surprisingly, after their slavery ended, only a remnant returned. There would be two more large returns and more would go home, but still, some remained.

In fairness, the situation in Jerusalem wasn't compatible with everyone returning at once, but history tells us that some embraced the Babylonian/Persian life and didn't return. Historians have also noted that many never lived in the land, so they lacked the same affection for the homeland as those who once did.

There have also been questions as to why Daniel didn't return. Perhaps age is the most contributing factor as it's estimated he would've been 80-85 years old. Another valid point made is that Daniel held a key place in the Persian government. We'll see later in the Book of Esther the importance of representatives for the Jews to be in such high places.

I raise the point of Daniel staying in his position of power to continue helping the cause of God's people because he was not alone. Thankfully, those like Mordecai and Esther were still in Persia.

Of others who didn't return, there was likely a mix of people who strategically needed to stay behind, but there were also those who'd embraced and preferred their life away from their Promised Land. In that, there was certainly a mix of those afraid to take a step and those who didn't want to give up what they'd come to love.

In New Testament terms, we'd say they loved the world.

Like Demas, who Paul writes about in 2 Timothy 4:10, who left "the work [mission]" because he loved the world.

As mentioned in the beginning, Ezra noted the ones who returned for Jerusalem were those whose hearts had been stirred by God.

No doubt, God was selecting and calling this remnant, but I can't help but think that some might have had their heart moved if they had been focused on the overall vision. Babylon was a temporary place of punishment. God wanted His people in the land He'd promised to them. I believe many lost the vision and let the distress of that day derail their previous calling or mission.

# NOW

Trials have a way of causing us to rethink callings and missions.

Personal changes.

National changes.

International changes.

These all present us with a proverbial fork in the road within our calling and mission. We can keep the vision and press on.

Maybe that fork in the road is a fair place to examine the calling; as we said on day one, check your ticket.

However, the vast majority of the time, God called you and gave you a specific mission knowing what specific trial was coming.

Therefore, we need to do as day two instructed—stick to our guns.

We need to keep the vision.

Some Jews kept the vision and their identity while in Babylon. This was difficult, but they continued. They didn't lose sight of what they were to do.

God isn't wishy-washy, neither is His plan, James wrote, "...**the Father ... does not change like shifting shadows" (James 1:17, NIV).**

# INSTRUCTION FOR UNCERTAIN TIMES:
## KEEP THE VISION

# 25

## SHINE

*From Daniel 6*
*Drawn from when God's people were subject to the Persians.*

# THEN

The Bible is full of stories recounting feats of God that just blow my mind—that's why we wrote the devotional book *Invincible*—but there are also aspects of the heroes of faith that amaze me. Nothing amazes me more than Daniel's faithful living while serving as a high-ranking government administrator in a deeply pagan empire—two pagan empires, for that matter.

How did Daniel walk this tightrope?

How did he do it so well?

How did he survive, much less distinguish himself above all others?

This particular accomplishment of Daniel's doesn't receive enough attention. There's not a better example of how to navigate a path to maintaining faithfulness amid national distress than Daniel's life and especially his career. That's why so many of our daily devotions focus on Daniel. There's also a reason Daniel lived a long life at the forefront of the most trying times of God's people.

We see Daniel's bureaucratic career begin when he was first deported with a few other select Jewish aristocratic young men into the royal court of King Nebuchadnezzar. From the very beginning, he navigated a path of holding on to the Law and excelling at his work. The first move he makes is choosing not to eat from the king's table, but rather to eat only vegetables and water. His actions proved to be excellent. Daniel, Hananiah, Mishael, and Azariah proved to be the top of their class.

Scripture records,

> *To these four young men God gave knowledge and understanding of all kinds of literature and learning. And Daniel could understand visions and dreams of all kinds. At the end of the time set by the king to bring them into his service, the chief official presented them to Nebuchadnezzar. The king talked with them, and he found none equal to Daniel, Hananiah, Mishael and Azariah; so they entered the king's service. In every matter of wisdom and understanding about which the king questioned them, he found them ten times better than all the magicians and enchanters in his whole kingdom* (Daniel 1: 17-20).

Daniel gained even higher esteem in Nebuchadnezzar's court after interpreting the dream of the statue for the king. He even was promoted to the third highest position in the Babylonian empire, but that post was short-lived because, a few hours later, the empire ended.

In an exceedingly rare move, Daniel was retained by the Persian king. Daniel 6 records how he rose to prominence again in the Persian Empire,

> *It pleased Darius to appoint 120 satraps to rule throughout the kingdom, with three administrators over them, one of whom was Daniel. The satraps were made accountable to them so that the king might not suffer loss. Now Daniel so distinguished himself among the administrators and the satraps by his exceptional qualities that the king planned to set him over the whole kingdom. At this, the administrators and the satraps tried to find grounds for charges against Daniel in his conduct of government affairs, but they were unable to do so. They could find no corruption in him, because he was trustworthy and neither corrupt nor negligent* (Daniel 6:1-4, NIV).

Under the Babylonian king and Persian kings, Daniel not only distinguished himself highly, but also, through his character and his career, he brought glory to God.

King Nebuchadnezzar proclaimed, "Surely your God is the God of gods and the Lord of kings and a revealer of mysteries, for you were able to reveal this mystery" (Daniel 2:47).

The Persian king even made a decree for the empire to worship Daniel's God,

> "I issue a decree that in every part of my kingdom people must fear and reverence the God of Daniel. For he is the living God and he endures forever; his kingdom will not be destroyed, his dominion will never end. He rescues

and he saves he performs signs and wonders in the heavens and on the earth. He has rescued Daniel from the power of the lions" (Daniel 6:26-27, NIV).

Don't miss this, and let it sink in: Even after being ripped away from his home and placed in a foreign land as a slave, Daniel excelled even more. In doing so he was able to cause two of the most powerful men in history to bow before God.

# NOW

As followers of Christ, this should be our desire for our lives every day. We should wish to live in such a way that points others to God, and even more so in uncertain times as everyone grasps for truth. Daniel's life is the blueprint. He exemplified what the Apostle Paul instructed the believers in Philippi, "…**become blameless and pure, children of God without fault in a warped and crooked generation. Then you will shine among them like stars in the sky" (Philippians 2:15, NIV).**

## INSTRUCTION FOR UNCERTAIN TIMES: SHINE

# 26

## IN UNCERTAIN TIMES
# KEEP UP YOUR SPIRITUAL DISCIPLINES

*From Daniel 6*
*Drawn from when God's people were subject to the Persians.*

# THEN

We've looked at a lot about Daniel's life so far and we haven't even discussed the quintessential Daniel story—Daniel and the lion's den. Even so, we touched on what led to Daniel being thrown in with the hungry lions. Daniel stood out and rose above his circumstances because of his integrity, work ethic and skills. Frankly, he "outshone" the others, and that intimidated fellow workers. In today's language, they couldn't handle him dominating the employee-of-the-month award. They wanted the front row parking spot for once. To say they were envious is an understatement.

This jealousy is recorded in Daniel 6,

> *Now Daniel so distinguished himself among the administrators and the satraps by his exceptional qualities that the king planned to set him over the whole*

*kingdom. At this, the administrators and the satraps tried to find grounds for charges against Daniel in his conduct of government affairs…* (Daniel 6:3-4).

Daniel's fellow administrators, and the satraps under his watch, attempted to gather dirt on Daniel but found none. They concluded the only way to find anything convicting required targeting his faith.

They devised a plan and coerced King Darius to issue a decree that no one could bow or pray to any other god but himself. Violators of the decree would be thrown into the den of lions. Under Persian law, a king's decree cannot be rescinded.

Next, they waited for Daniel to carry out his daily discipline. Each day he bowed and prayed with open windows in his upstairs rooms. He knew the decree, but he continued his daily spiritual discipline. They caught him in the act, praying for God to help him. He was arrested and brought to the king and ultimately thrown into the lion's den. An angel was sent by God to close the mouth of the lions. God saved Daniel like he'd saved Daniel's buddies, best known as Shadrach, Meshach, and Abednego.

Belief and allegiance to Yahweh were centered on Jerusalem and the Temple. Being uprooted and taken to a strange land, Daniel had an easy out—a pass, if you will—to become lax or less serious in his faith practices. When the decree was given, Daniel could've just taken a thirty-day prayer break. We do it. Don't we? Consider the 2020 COVID-19 crisis, where, along with the shutdown of church worship services, many have shut down the practice of their faith.

Not Daniel. To Daniel, his prayer time was his lifeline—essential to his daily life.

# NOW

When difficulties impose themselves upon our lives, it's tempting to throw our faith practices out the window, whether prayer, Bible reading, church, fasting, journaling, or whatever you do. Yet, it's in those difficult times we need to be one-on-one in the presence of God—even more so. It's in those times we need our faith strengthened and our hearts in tune with God.

I believe the context of Daniel 6 represents the right attitude of Daniel. In verse 11, it is said he was caught praying for strength. So, he risked his life to pray about strength to keep praying.

When difficulty comes, it's so easy to drop our guard and relax our disciplines, but it's in those times we need those disciplines the most—to draw us even closer to Him.

In the Book of Hebrews, we find a passage encouraging Christ-followers to continue meeting together. The verse focuses on the specific discipline of gathering as a body of believers, but I believe the principle rings true for all practices of our faith. Hebrews 10:24-25 says to not give up meeting even as *the Day* is approaching. *The day* is the Day of the Lord—the end times. The writer is speaking into an exact timing, but I think we also could easily see that qualifier of "as the Day is approaching" to be equivalent to when things become difficult. Some may stop meeting together under the threat of persecution, but God is clear. His people need the strength and encouragement of one another *especially* in times of persecution or under such a threat. Let's apply this verse to all spiritual disciplines. We must not stop our spiritual disciplines when times are uncertain, but instead, increase them with great intent and vigor. The writer of Hebrews wrote, **"And let us consider how we may spur one another on toward love and good deeds, not giving up meeting together, as some are in the habit of** doing, but encouraging one another—and all the more as you see the Day approaching" (Hebrews 10:24-25, NIV).

# INSTRUCTION FOR UNCERTAIN TIMES:
## KEEP UP YOUR SPIRITUAL DISCIPLINES

# 27
## IN UNCERTAIN TIMES
# GOD GIVES CRAZY DREAMS

*From Daniel 2, 4, 7 - 12*
*Drawn from when God's people were subject to the Persians.*

# THEN

By no means are we the first to work through Daniel's life to give guidance on how to live in difficult times. Daniel's life has stood as an example for 2,500 years. His example and the truths gleaned from his experience have been preached and written about time and time again. I know this to be true because I've heard such sermons and read such books. In the messages and books, I've seen that much is made over the narratives in his life.

This is what we've done so far.

We shared about Daniel's bold stance when he was first brought to the royal court.

We looked at how he interpreted King Nebuchadnezzar's dream.

We discussed the fiery furnace and the lions' den stories.

We even addressed the wild story of the handwriting on the wall causing the Babylonian king to freak out—and rightfully so, eh?

We've covered almost all the narratives in The Book of Daniel. They yield great truths for uncertain times.

We've been instructed to:

- Trust in God's Word
- Bet on God
- Be Willing to Burn
- Shine
- Keep Up Spiritual Disciplines

Great truths.

However, these truths only cover a third of the book.

The other two-thirds tell of dreams given to Daniel or those God used him to interpret. In this very uncertain time of captivity in Babylon, and living under Persian rule, God sent wild but meaningful dreams to Daniel.

This would also be true for his contemporaries, Jeremiah and Ezekiel.

This seems to always be the case. In the most difficult and darkest periods, God speaks the most. He never just tells of immediate troubles, but rather lifts the eyes of His people beyond the current valley onto the mountain peaks on the far horizon. In the most trying times, God provides the best glimpses of His Kingdom and eternity.

Let's just hit a quick overview of Daniel's experience.

In Daniel 2, God tells Daniel the dream King Nebuchadnezzar dreamed and gives him the interpretation. In this dream, God lists a succession of empires that will possess the land of Babylon from that point in history until the Messiah establishes His eternal kingdom. This shows Daniel immediately that the captivity in Babylon won't last forever, and it gives understanding for ages to come.

In Daniel 4, God uses Daniel to interpret other dreams of the king.

In Daniel 7 and 8, God gives Daniel his own dream that parallels and provides more insight into King Nebuchadnezzar's dream about the statue. Here, Daniel is given exact details of what will happen in the following empires of Persia and Greece.

In Daniel 9, he's given details of the timing of the coming of the Messiah, and the establishment of His Kingdom. He's even told how this age will end.

In Daniel 10, the angel Gabriel is sent to him to explain the dreams.

In Daniel 11, he's given insane details of events that'll happen.

In Daniel 12, he's given much more about how this age will end.

Daniel was given immense insight.

# NOW

Now, no one other than the Apostle John has received information at the level Daniel received. However, if you're seeking the Lord—if you're keeping up with your spiritual disciplines—I believe you must be ready and expectant for the Lord to reveal guidance to you in uncertain times.

We look at that idea as weird today, but that's how God works, and what He's done. Don't think it's strange, rather expect it and then accept it. The dream or other unique form of communication to you will be to encourage you and for you to use to encourage others.

This truth of dreams and visions being given in difficult times is a principle presented in Joel and then is repeated by the Apostle Peter in the Book of Acts. It speaks of dreams and visions being given in the last days. That is the true and chief meaning of the text, but I believe the passage could be understood as a blueprint for facing tough trials, for tough trials are what believers will face at the end of the age. Here's Peter quoting the Prophet Joel, **"'In the last days, God says, I will pour out my Spirit on all people. Your sons and daughters will prophesy, your young men will see visions, your old men will dream dreams. Even on my servants, both men and women, I will pour out my Spirit in those days, and they will prophesy" (Acts 2:17-18, NIV).**

# INSTRUCTION FOR UNCERTAIN TIMES:
## GOD GIVES CRAZY DREAMS

## 28

### IN UNCERTAIN TIMES

# RISE UP

*From Esther*
*Drawn from when God's people were subject to the Persians.*

# THEN

Haman, the highest-ranking official in the Persian Empire, convinced King Xeres to make a decree calling for the destruction of the Jewish people. A date was set, and couriers took the order across the empire calling for the destruction, murder, and annihilation of all Jews— young and old, women, and little children—everyone in one single day.

As we have already found with Daniel's arrest and his eventual punishment of being thrown in the Lion's Den, the Persian king's threats couldn't be rescinded.

On the 13th day of the month of Adar, God's people were scheduled to be erased from the Persian Empire.

In Esther 3:15, it's recorded that the capital city of Susa was "bewildered."

From all the cases we've shared of the national distress that ever befell God's people, this was the direst.

Decreed, signed, and sealed, destruction was coming to God's people. The circumstances appeared hopeless, but just as God always works—there was a plan in motion.

King Xeres had disposed of his queen and searched the empire over until he found a desirable replacement. We know her as Esther, and unbeknownst to the king, she was a Jew.

On hearing the decree, Mordecai, who had raised Esther, met with her to see if she would intercede on behalf of her people.

Going before the king to ask anything, much less challenge his decree, was dangerous—life-and-death dangerous.

Her reply to Mordecai is recorded in Esther 4:11, "All the king's officials and the people of the royal provinces know that for any man or woman who approaches the king in the inner court without being summoned the king has but one law: that they be put to death unless the king extends the gold scepter to them and spares their lives…"

In reply, Mordecai sent back this answer: "Do not think that because you are in the king's house you alone of all the Jews will escape. For if you remain silent at this time, relief and deliverance for the Jews will arise from another place, but you and your father's family will perish. And who knows but that you have come to your royal position for such a time as this?"

"For such a time as this."

"Who knows but that you have come to your royal position for such a time as this."

Yes.

And yes.

God had a plan.

He'd been working.

Though a decree had been made, He had planted Esther in the palace to plead for her people, but she would have to speak up.

She'd have to rise up.

She did, Haman ended up hanging, and her people were spared.

# NOW

In each case we've shared, though God allowed distress and calamity, He put people in place to reverse the dire circumstances.

As the Babylonians surrounded Jerusalem to destroy it, Jeremiah had been planted in the city. He was called to tell the people what God was doing. He had to speak and face the difficulties of that prophetic calling.

He had to rise up.

He did.

While the Jews were taken into captivity, God planted a fellow exile and called him to speak to them about what was going on, to call the people to repentance, and to give hope. Ezekiel had to speak and carry out this calling.

He had to rise up.

He did.

God allowed Babylon to destroy Jerusalem and the Temple. Though the people were carried off into exile, God allowed Daniel to be planted in the government and to rise to power. There's no doubt God used Daniel to do much for his people, but, again, it required boldness.

He had to rise up.

He did.

Though Haman sought to wipe out the Jews from the Persian Empire, God planted one of His own in the palace. Esther had been placed there for "such a time as this." Yet, she still had to risk her life to approach the king.

She had to rise up.

She did.

God has placed you where you are. He knew in advance what distress would come. He knew there would be uncertainty, but he has a plan. You are a part of that plan.

You may not be required to appear before a king, but you will be asked to rise up.

Just as Mordecai told Esther, **"…who knows but that you have come to your [current] position for such a time as this?" (Esther 4:12, NIV).**

# INSTRUCTION FOR UNCERTAIN TIMES:
## RISE UP

# DISTRESS IN THE RUINS

Week 5

# INTRODUCTION
# DISTRESS IN THE RUINS

**Uncertain times** had challenged the resolve of God's people more than anything they had faced, when a remnant returned to Jerusalem and Judea from Babylonian captivity following King Cyrus' decree.

God had relented and the exile was over.

He'd fulfilled the hope He'd promised through the prophets.

Once again God's people were back in the Promised Land.

They were home, but it wasn't the Kingdom they once knew.

God's people returned to ruins and ashes.

Centuries would pass before they returned to their original prosperity when King Nebuchadnezzar marched into Jerusalem.

This period of rebuilding the ruins of Jerusalem happened simultaneously with the previous section. As the majority of God's people continued in Persia, some returned to their homeland and set about the great work of starting again. Like the original exilic deportations, the return was comprised of a series of different returns, stretching over a one-hundred-year period.

Three main returns dominate the narrative of this time period. Sheshbazzar led the first group who returned, with the initial mission to rebuild the Temple. Notable names such as Zerubbabel, Joshua the high priest, Haggai, and Zechariah were in this first set of returnees.

Ezra led the second group, which focused on reform and revival.

Nehemiah, who was a contemporary of Ezra, came in the final notable return, and he led the rebuilding of the walls of Jerusalem.

Scripture tells the story of the return through the history books of Ezra and Nehemiah. These books occur over the same period as Esther, but Esther takes place back in Persia. It's also told through the postexilic prophets: Haggai, Zechariah, and Malachi.

Once again God's people found themselves in times that were difficult and uncertain.

What was God's people to do?

What would God do?

What was learned by God's people in this time stood as lessons for them for ages to come. These lessons still serve us today.

What can we learn to help us stand firm in national distress?

What can we learn of God to help us in times of chaos and difficulty?

# 29

IN  UNCERTAIN  TIMES
# GOD WILL RELENT BUT THERE MAY STILL BE A MESS

*From Ezra 1 - 3*
*Drawn from when God's people returned to a nation in ruins.*

## THEN

With King Cyrus' decree the captivity ended.

Sheshbazzar led the first group of returnees.

Psalm 126, believed to have been written at the time of the returns to Jerusalem, describes the joy of God relenting and the end of the exile.

> *When the Lord [brought back the captives to] Zion,*
> *we were like those who dreamed.*
> *Our mouths were filled with laughter,*
> *our tongues with songs of joy.*
> *Then it was said among the nations,*
> *"The Lord has done great things for them."*

151

*The Lord has done great things for us,*
 *and we are filled with joy.*
*[Bring back our captives] Lord,*
 *like streams in the Negev.*
*Those who sow with tears*
 *will reap with songs of joy.*
*Those who go out weeping,*
 *carrying seed to sow,*
*will return with songs of joy,*
 *carrying sheaves with them* (Psalm 126, NIV).

There was great joy in the return.

There was a pep in their step.

The long journey may have dampened that pep, but the sight they found in Jerusalem would have quenched their joy.

A description of what they found when they arrived is not given, but the prophet Micah, speaking 200 years before, foretold what they would find. Micah wrote, "Therefore because of you, Zion will be plowed like a field, Jerusalem will become a heap of rubble, the Temple hill a mound overgrown with thickets" (Micah 3:12).

Among the group of returnees, some had once lived in the land and others had only heard the stories.

The sight must have been overwhelming.

Again, we're not told exactly what they saw, but in Ezra 3, after the Temple was rebuilt, Ezra wrote:

> *And all the people gave a great shout of praise to the Lord, because the foundation of the house of the Lord was laid. But many of the older priests and Levites and family heads, who had seen the former temple, wept aloud when they saw the foundation of this temple being*

*laid, while many others shouted for joy. No one could distinguish the sound of the shouts of joy from the sound of weeping, because the people made so much noise. And the sound was heard far away* (Ezra 3:11-13).

The rebuilt Temple was such a poor shadow of Solomon's Temple that the people wept.

Jews returned home to a city in ruins, left desolate for fifty years at that point, leaving them to start from scratch. There were no homes. No Temple. No infrastructure. The remnant had to clear the rubble and rebuild.

It's been said that Judah was a kingdom when the people left but a colony when they returned.

Eighty years later, the cupbearer to the Persian king, Nehemiah, heard the report that the walls of Jerusalem remained in ruins and the gates had been burned. He would then lead an endeavor to rebuild the walls.

God relented on the punishment.

The difficulty came to pass, but a mess remained.

Returnees were tasked with physically rebuilding.

# NOW

As it has already been stated, not every time of personal or national distress is a punishment for sin.

But judgment does come.

The Assyrian invasion, the destruction of Jerusalem, and the Babylonian captivity comprised God's disciplinary response to sin.

The Egyptian bondage was not.

The later Greek and Roman occupation weren't necessarily due to sin. In any case, tribulations suffered due to sin, or merely from difficulty in a fallen world may still leave us to wade through a mess even though God may resolve and rescue us.

Often the joy of God's rescue is diminished due to the real-life chaos that continues even after the rescue. We must not lose heart over the remaining mess. In the case of completing the Temple, the people of God became discouraged. The prophet Haggai addresses the matter, and as mentioned, Nehemiah returned to find the walls left untouched, no doubt due to discouragement.

One of the major challenges for pursuing a faithful life in uncertain times is that although God is with us, the mission before us can be discouraging. The Apostle Paul addressed this in the epistle to the Galatians, **"Let us not become weary in doing good, for at the proper time we will reap a harvest if we do not give up" (Galatians 6:9, NIV).**

# INSTRUCTION FOR UNCERTAIN TIMES: GOD WILL RELENT BUT THERE STILL MAY BE A MESS

# 30

## IN UNCERTAIN TIMES
# GOD ALWAYS GIVES HOPE

*From Ezra 1 - 3*
*Drawn from when God's people returned to a nation in ruins.*

# THEN

In many of the devotions, we have alluded to the hope God gives even in difficult times like the exile to Babylon.

He does.

This is seen in almost all the prophet's writings.

Jeremiah and Ezekiel both show this.

Think how remarkable this reality is.

God calls Jeremiah and Ezekiel to speak to His people about why He is punishing them. They pronounce the sentencing and tell of the hardships ahead. The two stress God's anger and the people's need for repentance, but amid enacting judgment, God still gives hope.

After Jeremiah relayed God's anger for the unfaithfulness of Judah, he went on to speak on behalf of the Lord. He said, and later wrote, "'Return, faithless Israel,' declares the Lord, 'I will frown on you no longer, for I am faithful,' declares the Lord, 'I will not be angry forever'" (Jeremiah 3:12).

This is common throughout the prophets. Their messages express God's anger, pronounce judgment, and always weave in a message of hope.

God speaks through Jeremiah about Judah's eventual return. This is pronounced even before they're in exile. Jeremiah spoke and wrote, "At that time they will call Jerusalem The Throne of the Lord, and all nations will gather in Jerusalem to honor the name of the Lord. No longer will they follow the stubbornness of their evil hearts. In those days, the people of Judah will join the people of Israel, and together they will come from a northern land to the land I gave your ancestors as an inheritance" (Jeremiah 3:17-18, NIV).

As you can see, this message of hope comes only three chapters into the fifty-one chapters of the Book of Jeremiah. This cycle repeats throughout the entire book as it does in Isaiah and the other prophets.

Ezekiel reflects this same cycle within the book that bears his name. Ezekiel speaks and writes, "This is what the Sovereign Lord says: 'I will gather you from the nations and bring you back from the countries where you have been scattered, and I will give you back the land of Israel again. They will return to it and remove all its vile images and detestable idols. I will give them an undivided heart and put a new spirit in them; I will remove from them their heart of stone and give them a heart of flesh'" (Ezekiel 11:17-18, NIV).

We bring this aspect of hope to light because this is God.

As we read in a previous devotion, though God punishes sin, He prefers to show His people mercy and love.

Not only did the prophets give words of encouragement, but these words came to pass. God's people had the opportunity to leave the foreign lands and return home. They rebuilt Jerusalem and the nation out of the rubble. Life once again flourished there.

The words of the prophets rang true.

156

God gathered them and brought them home. He always gives hope.

# NOW

In whatever we may face personally, or collectively as a nation, God will have hope to foretell and eventually give to us. The testimony of the message of the prophets shows this over and over and the witness of history proves their words.

If you look closer to the passages about returning quoted above from Jeremiah and Ezekiel, you'll see God wasn't just talking about the return from the exile to Babylon. The original hearers were meant to understand God would do those things, but God is speaking of another scattering and gathering that will happen. This scattering happened in 70 A.D. at the hands of the Romans. The fulfillment of the gathering happens at the end of the age and leads to the ultimate hope for God's people—the Kingdom of Heaven.

No matter what we face, there will always be future hope promised. When that future hope is reached, we are relieved of the need for future hopes because we will be living in the New Heaven and New Earth in perfect glorified bodies. At that time, we will experience perfection in God's presence, and we will have eternal life.

One of the major challenges for pursuing a faithful life in uncertain times is that, although God is with us, the mission before us can be discouraging. The Apostle Paul addressed this in the epistle to the Galatians, **"God's dwelling place is now among the people, and he will dwell with them. They will be his people, and God himself will be with them and be their God. 'He will wipe every tear from their eyes. There will be no more death or mourning or crying or pain, for the old order of things has passed away'" (Revelation 21:2-4, NIV).**

# INSTRUCTION FOR UNCERTAIN TIMES:
## GOD ALWAYS GIVES HOPE

# 31
## IN UNCERTAIN TIMES
# KEEP FIRST THINGS FIRST

*From Ezra 1 – 3, Haggai 1*
*Drawn from when God's people returned to a nation in ruins.*

# THEN

Judah's time in exile was meant to be a time of discipline.

The purpose of discipline isn't only punitive, also it is meant to produce growth and change. Idolatry and failure to honor God's law led to exile. One would think that God's people would have gone overboard in their efforts to be faithful to Him. Perhaps that was the desire of their hearts when they first returned, but that desire waned.

In pursuing faithfulness to God, the Temple was a key component, which is why the focus of the first group's return to Jerusalem was to rebuild it. This task dominates Ezra's account of this first return.

Within King Cyrus' decree to release the Jews, he includes the building of the Temple. Jews who planned to stay in Babylon were instructed to still give a freewill offering to help with the rebuilding. Cyrus even gave the group's leader, Sheshbazzar, the articles previously taken from the Temple by King Nebuchadnezzar.

The effort was made to assemble priests, Levites, singers, gatekeepers, and Temple servants to all return in that first group. The first tasks were to rebuild the altar and lay the Temple's foundation.

By the emphasis placed on it in Scripture, it's evident that rebuilding the Temple was central to the return, and it appears that everyone made that a priority, initially.

Twenty years after the return, one of the returnees was given a message from God.

Haggai was told to address the people because they'd abandoned the priority of rebuilding the Temple and focused on their own homes and lives. He preached:

> *This is what the Lord Almighty says: "These people say, 'The time has not yet come to rebuild the Lord's house.'"*
>
> *Then the word of the Lord came through the prophet Haggai: "Is it a time for you yourselves to be living in your paneled houses, while this house remains a ruin?" Now this is what the Lord Almighty says: "Give careful thought to your ways. You have planted much, but harvested little. You eat, but never have enough. You drink, but never have your fill. You put on clothes, but are not warm. You earn wages, only to put them in a purse with holes in it." This is what the Lord Almighty says: "Give careful thought to your ways. ⁸ Go up into the mountains and bring down timber and build my house, so that I may take pleasure in it and be honored," says the Lord. "You expected much, but see, it turned out to be little. What you brought home; I blew away. Why?" declares the Lord Almighty. "Because of my house, which remains a ruin, while each of you is busy*

160

*with your own house. Therefore, because of you, the heavens have withheld their dew and the earth its crops. I called for a drought on the fields and the mountains, on the grain, the new wine, the olive oil and everything else the ground produces, on people and livestock, and on all the labor of your hands"* (Haggai 2:1-11, NIV).

The people of God who returned meant well, but their focus turned to building their own homes and lives while the Temple lay unfinished. In verse two, we see they claimed the time hadn't come for them to finish it. They gave excuses. Regardless of the difficulty they faced, they had not prioritized God.

Without the Temple complete, they likely weren't fully carrying out all the Law.

Haggai shares that the reason for their new difficulties with drought, famine, and trying times, are because they failed to put first things first.

They failed to put God first.

# NOW

Duh. Putting God first is not a new concept.

However, there's a real struggle in understanding how to balance placing God first and doing the things in life we must do to survive.

We're not sure if focusing on their own needs rather than the Temple was consciously rebellious or if the people truly thought once they finished their homes, they'd begin on the Temple. Likely, they didn't realize twenty years had passed.

Remember they found Jerusalem in rubble when they returned.

They had no homes.

161

There was no infrastructure.

It makes sense they pursued these things, but in the economy of God, prioritizing Him as number one would naturally lead them to acquire all the things they needed. When we're in uncertain times we can easily wear the same blinders. Yes, we need to attend to daily life, but still, we must put God first. We need to remember Jesus' words, "**Seek first his kingdom and his righteousness, and all these things will be given to you as well" (Matthew 6:33, NIV).**

# INSTRUCTION FOR UNCERTAIN TIMES:
## KEEP FIRST THINGS FIRST

# 32
## IN UNCERTAIN TIMES
# STAY IN THE WORD

*From Ezra 7, Nehemiah 8*
*Drawn from when God's people returned to a nation in ruins.*

# THEN

Thirty-five years before the destruction of Jerusalem, there's a remarkable story from the reign of Josiah that helps us understand how Judah strayed so far from God. While making repairs in the Temple as part of Josiah's reforms, they found something that had been missing—The Book of the Law.

The Torah.

God's Word.

Yes, for some period of time, the Book of the Law had been lost.

Now, there were certainly some who knew the message by heart because most learned it orally.

However, for people who were instructed to live according to the Law, the Book was missing, and somehow no one knew it was missing.

This shows the unfortunate lack of value they placed on the Word of God, which ultimately led to idolatry and then to exile.

The strange saga also shows the importance of leaders keeping the Word of God before His people.

With the backdrop of this story, I find Ezra's role in the return from exile especially interesting. Ezra and Nehemiah were contemporaries. Biblical background scholar Thomas Briscoe writes that "the efforts of Ezra and Nehemiah saved the Jewish community from extinction. New foundations of the Jews were laid for the physical and spiritual well-being of the Jewish community."[1]

He stresses the importance of Ezra and Nehemiah's roles, considering them to be as vital as Esther's.

These two men's faithfulness and obedience to God played a major role in the rebuilding. We'll talk about Nehemiah extensively. His leadership projected and protected God's people in Jerusalem.

Ezra was a leader, but his major contribution was keeping the Word of God before the people. The Book of Ezra shares about his heart and knowledge of the Word with phrases like:

"Ezra...was a teacher well versed in the Law of Moses" (Ezra 7:6, NIV).

"The gracious hand of God was on him. For Ezra had devoted himself to the study and observance of the Law of the Lord, and to teaching its decrees and laws in Israel" (Ezra 7:9-10, NIV).

Ezra was granted the task of taking another group of returnees to Jerusalem. Although he was appointed to lead, his main role was to make sure the people carried out the Law of God.

He did this.

Nehemiah records a gathering of the Jews in the land for eight days of reading the Law and teaching. Ezra led with other priests. The

---

[1] Briscoe, Thomas V. *Holman Bible Atlas: A Complete Guide to the Expansive Geography of Biblical History.* Broadman & Holman, 1999.

Bible says, "They read from the Book of the Law of God, making it clear and giving the meaning so that the people understood what was being read" (Nehemiah 8:8, NIV). From this teaching Nehemiah records there was great joy, "because they now understood the words that had been made known to them."

This focus on the Word of God led to repentance and, ultimately, revival. Historians view this as helping the Jewish people keep their religious identity throughout the restoration of the land.

Ezra stayed in the Word and helped the nation stay in the Word.

# NOW

I wonder if we live like the nation before Josiah found the missing Book of the Law. I feel we continue living our lives the way we want as if God hadn't already spoken.

With the access we have to Bible translations and Bible study tools, it seems impossible we'd ever "lose" the Word, but today in the United States, Christians are more biblically illiterate than at any time in history. We've lost it.

In a time of ease, we've moved away from the Word. I'm concerned about what will happen in the future when life in these times become even more difficult. I fear we will forsake the study of the Word.

We must stay in the Word.

We must lean on the instruction the Lord gave Joshua as he headed into trying and uncertain times, **"Keep this Book of the Law always on your lips; meditate on it day and night, so that you may be careful to do everything written in it. Then you will be prosperous and successful" (Joshua 1:8, NIV).**

# INSTRUCTION FOR UNCERTAIN TIMES:
## STAY IN THE WORD

# 33
## IN UNCERTAIN TIMES
# KEEP DREAMING

*From Nehemiah 1 - 2*
*Drawn from when God's people returned to a nation in ruins.*

# THEN

Nearly a hundred years after the first group returned to Jerusalem, Nehemiah, who was the king's cupbearer, received a visit from his brother from Judah. Nehemiah asked about the city. His brother reported that the remnant now living back in the land was in trouble. The walls of Jerusalem still lay in ruins and the gates lay burnt. This left the people in the city exposed.

Upon hearing this news, Nehemiah was heart-broken. Scripture says he wept and mourned, and then fasted and prayed.

During his time of fasting and prayer, Nehemiah dreamed a dream.

His heart for his fellow people caused him to wish the wall could be rebuilt and through that heart he dreamed of going to rebuild the walls.

He prayed for God's favor.

Soon after, God gave him the opening he needed. The king noticed Nehemiah's sadness and inquired. Nehemiah again prayed and then requested to be sent to rebuild the walls.

God's favor certainly was on Nehemiah and his dream. The Persian king granted his request. He also gave him protection for his travel and timber for the gates.

Nehemiah then left for Judah.

There he rallied the people of God to rebuild the walls. During the process, they met much resistance, but Nehemiah pushed and pushed the people.

He dreamed a dream for God.

He didn't just dream, but he put feet to those dreams.

He accomplished the mission.

# NOW

We dream dreams for all aspects of our lives.

We dream about what we want to accomplish in our careers, hobbies, and homes.

We dream about our relationships and what we want them to be, and what we want for our kids.

We dream about vacations and larger, more stylish vehicles.

We dream dreams for all aspects of life, but we don't tend to dream big dreams for God. That's a shame. For, more than anything, we should dream about how we can make His name great and help others come to repentance.

Take note, though, our dreams may not always be what God wants for us. This happens in 2 Samuel 7, where King David dreams of building a Temple for God. David realizes he has a palace, but the place of God's special presence is still the temporary tabernacle. The king pursues that dream, but Nathan the prophet is sent to dial him back. He tells David that not he, but his son, will build the Temple. Yet, David still gathers all the supplies he can.

We, too, need to dream for God. If He redirects us, we'll still end up accomplishing something for Him.

First, we need to begin to dream dreams for God, then put feet to those dreams. Be warned, though, that in times of tribulation it's easy to be thrown off the dream(s) to focus on survival. Distress dampens our dreams, but only if we allow it. Be aware, when we find ourselves in the darkest times is when we need to dream the most.

Nehemiah accomplished many amazing things throughout his mission to rebuild the wall, but it all started with him dreaming a dream for God. At this point in history, it would have been easy to dismiss any ideas or dreams of doing something for God, but dreaming was most assuredly needed.

No matter how trying times become, we should always set our eyes on, and dream for, the eternal. The Apostle Paul wrote, **"So we fix our eyes not on what is seen, but on what is unseen, since what is seen is temporary, but what is unseen is eternal" (2 Corinthians 4:18, NIV).**

# INSTRUCTION FOR UNCERTAIN TIMES: KEEP DREAMING

# 34
## IN UNCERTAIN TIMES
# BOLDLY ASK

*From Nehemiah 1 - 3*
*Drawn from when God's people returned to a nation in ruins.*

# THEN

Nehemiah didn't merely dream for the Lord—He put feet to his dreams.

He saw the need within the mission of God. Jerusalem needed walls. He acted.

The first step of action he took was to pray. He prayed and fasted. His fasting needs to be seen as an extension of his praying. Fasting for God to intercede or give an answer is an expression of faith and an extension of our seriousness in asking of the Lord.

Think back to how many times this truth has come up in our study:

- In uncertain times cry out to God.
- In uncertain times pray.
- In uncertain times God hears.
- In uncertain times God answers.

Scriptural evidence makes clear—our first step should be to ask God for what we need, or for what we must do.

Jesus said, "You have not because you ask not."

We're to ask our Heavenly Father.

We're to echo the Israelites in Egypt who cried out to God.

We're to follow the footsteps of Hezekiah who took the letter from the Assyrian king, laid it out before the Lord, and asked for help.

Nehemiah prayed for God's favor. Quickly, that favor came when Nehemiah was allowed to speak candidly to the king. In Nehemiah 2:4, before he even responded to the king, Nehemiah prayed again for favor.

The second step of action Nehemiah took was to approach the king with a request. Much like Esther's danger in going before the king, Nehemiah's life was in danger as well. Just as the salvation from tribulation in Esther's day required the king's favor, so did Nehemiah's mission. He couldn't remedy the wall problem alone. He needed the authority the king could give to the endeavor. Fortifying the city apart from the king's permission would've been viewed as a threat to the Empire. Nehemiah also needed the protection the king gave along with the timber he provided.

For the mission to succeed, Nehemiah had to ask—boldly ask.

The asking didn't stop in the royal court either. When Nehemiah arrived in Jerusalem, he had to ask the people to help. He constantly had to ask of the people.

Nehemiah knew the necessity of the project.

Like Esther, Nehemiah was in that position "for such a time as this."

And, like Esther, he had to boldly ask.

# NOW

In challenging times, problems will be beyond our control; we won't be able to solve them alone.

In such times we cannot fly solo. We need to work with others.

We must develop the reflex to first ask in prayer.

Then, as the mission requires or as the Spirit leads, we must occasionally boldly ask others, even others in positions of power, for what we need to do God's will.

Nehemiah asked on so many levels. He asked the king for permission. He asked leaders in Jerusalem to listen. He asked for help to do the work. As problems persisted, he constantly asked for help. The need and mission demanded it.

We must realize when the need and mission outweigh whatever fear we might hold in asking. We need to remember Jesus' words, "**Do not be afraid of those who kill the body but cannot kill the soul. Rather, be afraid of the One who can destroy both soul and body in hell**" (Matthew 10:28, NIV).

## INSTRUCTION FOR UNCERTAIN TIMES:
### BOLDLY ASK

# 35

## IN UNCERTAIN TIMES
# BUST YOUR BUTT

*From Nehemiah 2 – 6*
*Drawn from when God's people returned to a nation in ruins.*

# THEN

Reading through the book of Nehemiah will exhaust you. Not because it's long or because of the writing. It's exhausting because Nehemiah hits the ground running to fulfill the mission to rebuild the walls of Jerusalem. He plows through full force and attacks the problem with insane intensity.

In the Scriptural narrative, problems constantly arise and challenge the work, but Nehemiah leads on. You can't help but cheer for the building of the wall because of how hard everyone is working and how persistent Nehemiah is in the task.

Listen to some of the descriptions of the intensity of the work throughout the rebuilding project.

"For the people worked with all their heart (Nehemiah 4:6, NIV)."

"The strength of the labors were giving out [due to the intensity]" (Nehemiah 4:10, NIV).

"Worked from first light of dawn till the stars came out" (Nehemiah 4:21, NIV).

"The wall was completed...in fifty-two days. When all our enemies heard about this, all the surrounding nations were afraid and lost their self-confidence, because they realized that this work had been done with the help of our God" (Nehemiah 6:15-16, NIV).

The people of God busted their butts to get the wall done.

And it's not like they had fifty-two smooth, perfect workdays.

Issues constantly arose.

Along with being the Jerusalem wall project manager, Nehemiah was commissioned by the king to be governor of Judah. Fellow governors of nearby provinces harassed the people of God.

First, Nehemiah and the Jewish wall builders faced insults. They grew weary and overwhelmed. Insults were followed by death threats. The people rose to the challenge when they received word that their enemies were planning to kill them as they worked.

Nehemiah wrote about their solution to this threat:

> *From that day on, half of my men did the work, while the other half were equipped with spears, shields, bows and armor. The officers posted themselves behind all the people of Judah who were building the wall. Those who carried materials did their work with one hand and held a weapon in the other, and each of the builders wore his sword at his side as he worked. But the man who sounded the trumpet stayed with me. Then I said to the nobles, the officials and the rest of the people, "The work is extensive and spread out, and we are widely separated from each other along the wall. Wherever you hear the sound of the trumpet, join us there. Our God will fight for us!" (Nehemiah 4:16-20).*

With a trowel in one hand and a sword in the other, they worked. Even in challenging situations, they pushed through.

They exemplified "pray like it all depends on you and work like it all depends on God."

They busted their butts.

# NOW

Why did they work so hard and fast?

Because they knew danger was coming. If the walls weren't up, all the rebuilding work in the city would have been done in vain.

Nehemiah had a God-placed urgency for this need. Fortunately, the people of Jerusalem responded and heard his appeal. This is rarely the case. Often, like with many of the accounts of the prophets, messages of urgency fell on deaf ears.

As followers of Christ, we have a mission—the Great Commission. We're called to make disciples all over the world. Within that mission, which all believers have, God gives us sub-callings in which we carry out our specific role within the Great Commission. Let's be honest, we don't often bust our butts on that mission, even in easy conditions. Therefore, when difficulty comes on us personally or within our nation, we tend to shelve our callings and the mission. We just try to survive and keep our heads above water. Interestingly, in chapter 5 of Nehemiah, the workers on the wall begin to fall away because they are forced to focus on survival. Nehemiah immediately springs into action and solves the problem, but the same sorts of challenges from this story can happen to us.

It's in those challenging times that we need to step up our game regarding the Great Commission. Those tough times often indicate an even harder time to share the Gospel awaits just around the corner. Therefore, we must take advantage of each opportunity before us.

Jesus shared this urgency we must possess for the Great Commission, He taught, "**As long as it is day, we must do the works of him who sent me. Night is coming, when no one can work**" (John 9:4, NIV).

# INSTRUCTION FOR UNCERTAIN TIMES:
## BUST YOUR BUTT

# OUR WORLD

# DISTRESS
# NOW&
# THEN

Week 6
## INTRODUCTION
# DISTRESS NOW & THEN

**Uncertain times** are always going to come for God's people. The time periods covered in this devotional book aren't exhaustive by any means. We could have discussed the Seleucids and Romans, another couple of foreign powers that occupied Israel. Next, we could've listed the challenges Christians have faced.

In the first century, Christians faced persecution from unbelieving Jews. For the first three centuries, Christians were fiercely persecuted by the Roman empire. Believers experienced atrocity after atrocity. Persecution hasn't ever ceased for them and has reared its head many times.

Right now, groups that track Christian persecution around the world say there are more Christians persecuted currently than at any point in history. According to prophecy, as the end of the age draws near, persecution will only grow worse and worse.

Beyond the outright persecution of God's people, there have always been believers living in nations that are in distress.

The distress can come from government oppression.

It can come from outside nations or from inner civil war.

National struggle can be financial. It can be an issue of famine, drought, disaster, or sickness.

In this fallen world something is always happening.

Throughout each daily devotion so far, all have been structured to reflect on the *then* so that we will have truth and instruction for *now*. We hope you've gained that truth, but it's not meant to be mere head knowledge. Rather, the bridge between the *then* and *now* exists to help you remain faithful in the *now* and *then*.

For whatever struggle we face or whatever national distress we will face, we need to lean on what we've learned from *then* and apply it to *now* and the *future*.

Mark it, we'll face difficult and uncertain times.

So, now let's consider, what will we as God's people do?

What will God do?

What have we learned from God's people for now and for the challenges ahead?

What have we learned to help us stand firm in national distress?

What will God do to help us in times of chaos and difficulty?

## 36

IN UNCERTAIN TIMES

# REPENT

*From Romans 3 – 10*
*Drawn from the truths presented in this book that have been*
*gathered from the instruction and example of God's people facing*
*great challenges.*

# THEN

Out of the forty truths presented in this book, this one should have been first. For in uncertain times and in times of distress—repent.

We've saved this truth for this section because we want to be clear: this truth wasn't just what Israel needed to do in the past but is what we need to do in the present. It's what we need to relay to future generations, for them to practice in the future.

The solution for all the troubled times touched upon in this book could have been repentance.

Repentance is the first action we should take.

Repentance is how we resolve, survive, or prosper in trying times.

Yet, our natural reaction is to fight and resist repentance.

In nearly every event retold in this book, there was resistance or complete avoidance of repentance.

Multiple times throughout these devotions we've looked at how God warned His people that if they didn't obey His commands, He'd exile them from the land. Time after time, they ignored those warnings. God was patient, but eventually, He pulled the proverbial trigger and brought punishment.

Alongside those many warnings, stretching from the first giving of the Law up to the Babylonian siege, were promises of provision for their sin. Repeatedly God told His people even if they sinned and turned toward idols, if they'd repent and return to Him, He'd forgive them.

One such time was in the life of Solomon, after the dedication celebration of the new Temple. The Lord appeared and said, "When I shut up the heavens so that there is no rain, or command locusts to devour the land or send a plague among my people, if my people, who are called by my name, will humble themselves and pray and seek my face and turn from their wicked ways, then I will hear from heaven, and I will forgive their sin and will heal their land" (2 Chronicles 7:13-14). In times of distress, especially when due to sin, God tells us to humble ourselves, repent of our sin, and turn back to Him. When we do, He will begin to remedy the trouble.

When trials are the result of sin, and repentance brings those trials or punishment to an end, a mess and consequences may remain. But, even if the difficulty had nothing to do with sin, it's still a circumstance that should bring us to our knees.

In Egypt, the Israelites were facing oppression, not because of sin, but they still "cried out" to God. The distress brought them to pursue God, and, because they pursued Him, He rescued them.

During the Assyrian invasion, the Northern Kingdom's ten tribes didn't repent, and the nation was destroyed. The people were carried away to exile. When Sennacherib campaigned through Judah, after trying every method to handle things in his own strength, Hezekiah finally humbled himself and prayed for God to help.

And God helped.

In Babylon, a remnant turned back to God. In the Book of Daniel, Daniel prays a prayer of repentance for the nation.

In Persia, Nehemiah's prayer before asking the king for permission to rebuild the walls began with a prayer of repentance.

In the ruins of Jerusalem, the people repented multiple times. Haggai called them to repent over failing to complete the Temple and placing their desires ahead of God. Ezra brought repentance in reading the Word. Unlike most of Israel's history, the people responded to the pre-exilic prophets.

Humbling ourselves and repenting is hard, but calamity can serve to trigger our return to God. In the Book of Revelation, it's amazing that even after horrific tribulation impacts the earth, people won't repent. This is repeated throughout the Book of Revelation.

We must build in this reflex—the reflex to repent.

# NOW

All trials and calamity are a fork in the proverbial road.

They create that intersection of which Robert Frost penned in "The Road Not Taken."

Uncertain times can either push us closer to God or further away. Rarely can someone remain unmoved or neutral in a crisis. Ahead of impending trials, we must make up our minds and train our hearts to turn back to God.

## National Repentance

When a tribulation is on a national level, an entire nation can repent. In the Book of Jonah, we see the pagan nation of Assyria has nationwide repentance. This can happen, but it's a rare thing. So, when a faithful remnant lives in a nation receiving calamity due to sin, it's tempting to throw one's hands up and say, "Let it burn." That's not the heart we should have. Though we may not be able to sway a nation, our hearts need to be broken in knowing what is at stake. We also still need to turn to God. In our personal repentance, we can trigger others to repent through our example. There are also cases in Scripture where the prayers of one intercessory person saved a nation.

Abraham's prayer for Sodom saved his nephew Lot.

Moses' prayers for Israel, on multiple occasions, saved them.

Hezekiah's prayer saved Jerusalem from the Assyrians.

It seems Daniel's prayer brought the relent of the Babylonian captivity.

Though our nation may be crumbling to the ground, as long as there is breath in our lungs, we must intercede. Not so much for the nation itself, but for the souls within her.

## Individual Repentance

This truth—the need for repentance—stands for our personal trials as well. Every struggle should bring us back to the Lord whether it's due to sin or not.

First, we must be sure we've come to salvation in repentance. We must all have a point in our lives where we realize that we're sinners and can't save ourselves from the ultimate punishment for sin—Hell. In this, we must also come to know that though God is love, and He does not want to sentence us to Hell, God is also just, which means He must punish sin. Fortunately, this struggle is resolved in Jesus dying for our sin on the cross. The penalty has been paid, but we must take hold of it by repenting and accepting that gift by faith.

This is salvation.

This is being born again.

This is receiving forgiveness for our sin.

This is receiving eternal life.

This must happen in our lives.

Praise the Lord for the struggles in life that bring us to the point of salvation.

Second, though we're saved, our battle with sin and tendency to drift from God remains. We should improve in our battle with sin, and grow in faithfulness throughout our lives, but there will always remain a struggle. Yet, God still allows us to turn from that sin and receive forgiveness. The Apostle John writes about this in his first epistle, **"If we confess our sins, he is faithful and just and will forgive us our sins and purify us from all unrighteousness" (1 John 1:9, NIV).**

We can't emphasize the importance of repentance enough.

Like the instruction from the first devotion, in uncertain times, we need to check our ticket. Almost always we'll see that we need to draw closer to God. It may not always reveal sin, for not every trial is a result of sin. It's OK to conclude you haven't sinned, but before you settle that issue, ask God to search your heart and reveal any sin. We have a way of tricking ourselves.

# INSTRUCTION FOR UNCERTAIN TIMES: REPENT

# 37
## IN UNCERTAIN TIMES
# STAY IN STEP
# WITH THE SPIRIT

*From John 14 & 16, Galatians 5*
*Drawn from the truths presented in this book that have been*
*gathered from the instruction and example of God's people facing*
*great challenges.*

# THEN

In Egypt, the Israelites knew to cry out to God for help. Moses was brave and bold enough to do what God called him to do.

During the Assyrian invasion, Isaiah kept his calling, and bravely told the king to not make treaties. Hezekiah was willing to pray.

During the Babylonian invasion, Jeremiah preached fearlessly and suffered while carrying out the will of God.

In Babylon, Daniel and the three Hebrew amigos remained faithful and shone through terrifying adversity. Shadrach, Meshach, and Abednego didn't bow to the idol and bravely faced the fiery furnace. Ezekiel was faithful and bold enough to carry out all he was asked to do—no matter how crazy the task.

Under Persian rule, Daniel continued to shine. He didn't stop praying and trusted God to take care of him in the lions' den. Esther bravely rose and was used to save her people.

In Jerusalem among the rubble, Nehemiah busted his butt. Ezra kept the word before the people. Haggai obeyed God.

Of course, this study has only focused on a portion of the history in the Bible. There are many more heroes of the faith. These men and women truly stood firm in uncertain times, but as believers today, we are much more equipped than they were. We can faithfully strive and navigate uncertain times far better than they even could dream of doing—for we have God inside of us.

At salvation, the Holy Spirit comes and dwells within us.

This wasn't the case for God's people before the Day of Pentecost.

Before Jesus was arrested, then went to the cross, the tomb, and ultimately ascended to Heaven, He told the disciples it was better for them that He go, rather than stay. That sounds crazy, but Jesus promised once He left, He'd send the Holy Spirit.

Each of us has the Holy Spirit indwelling us.

Jesus told them that the Holy Spirit would, "Teach you all things and will remind you of everything I have said" (John 14:26, NIV).

The Holy Spirit who indwells us teaches us.

Jesus also said, "He will guide you into all the truth. He will not speak on his own; he will speak only what he hears, and he will tell you what is yet to come. He will glorify me because it is from me that he will receive what he will make known to you. All that belongs to the Father is mine. That is why I said the Spirit will receive from me what he will make known to you" (John 16:13-15).

This means for all of life we have God the Holy Spirit living within us. He's teaching and guiding us. Elsewhere we read that He comforts and convicts. We also read that He'll illuminate and empower us. We're far more equipped than anyone who's excelled in uncertain times, because if we have the Holy Spirit in all times, then we have Him in uncertain times. This should give us immense peace and relief. We're never going to be left alone to fend for ourselves in difficult trials, nationally or personally.

# NOW

Though the Holy Spirit indwells us, His influence and empowerment aren't automatic. To some degree, yes, but we need to give Him control.

In Galatians 5, we read of the famed Fruit of the Spirit. The fruit is love, joy, peace, patience, kindness, goodness, faithfulness, gentleness, and self-control. There's no doubt these are noble behaviors we should desire to possess, but contrary to most teachings on this list, never once are believers told to act on their own power to acquire these virtues. Rather, in context, these are automatic results of the Holy Spirit's work in our life, and they don't automatically pop-up if we're not pursuing God. We don't develop the fruit if we're not walking with Him.

The Apostle Paul says the key to obtaining this fruit in your life is to, **"Keep in step with the Spirit" (Galatians 5:25, NIV).**

In uncertain times especially, we need the comfort and guidance of the Holy Spirit, therefore, we must keep in step with Him. And doing these daily devotionals is a great start to staying in step with Him. We stay in step by spending regular time seeking God.

We seek Him in prayer. Not just in making requests, but in a two-way conversation. We also must be in His Word.

By faithfully and consistently spending this time seeking God, He'll give us steps to take. To stay in step with Him, we need to obey. When we take a step of obedience, eventually another step will be shown to us. We'll then stay in step with the Holy Spirit.

# INSTRUCTION FOR UNCERTAIN TIMES:
## STAY IN THE STEP WITH THE SPIRIT

# 38

# MAKE DISCIPLES

*From Matthew 28, Acts 1*
*Drawn from the truths presented in this book that have been*
*gathered from the instruction and example of God's people facing*
*great challenges.*

# THEN

The twelve disciples received a unique calling in being Jesus' chosen twelve, but they also were forerunners of all who follow Jesus.

We're called to do what they did. When Jesus called them, He gave them only one task—to fish for men.

One task—to share the Gospel.

One task—to make disciples.

They were to fish for souls.

The task for us and them is streamlined into just one thing.

Jesus makes it even more clear in Matthew 28:19-20—The Great Commission. He says, "Therefore go and make disciples of all nations, baptizing them in the name of the Father and of the Son and of the Holy Spirit, and teaching them to obey everything I have commanded you."

This is our mission.

This is our calling.

195

Simple.

The first disciples took this seriously and gave their lives to it.

As Jesus said in Acts 1:8, they became His witnesses in Jerusalem, Judea, Samaria, and to the ends of the earth. Historians write that these twelve men turned the world upside down, set it on fire.

Thousands became disciples in their generation, directly because of the original twelve's witness and efforts. The millions who have come to Christ since is in large part because of the disciples.

If we followed the fishing analogy Jesus used, the disciples took home an unbelievable haul.

If He meant the analogy in comparison to "commercial fishing" (which is what the disciples knew), if their success as fishers of men was in the field of commercial fishing, these men made incalculable fortunes. They would've built the largest fishing operation in the world.

If the illustration was made towards someone fishing for a fish fry, as we do down here in the south, then they could've fed their whole town many times over.

If the analogy was aimed at tournament fishing (which is what I enjoy) then they broke records and won all the accolades. They'd have their own fishing shows and lines of products. I imagine Peter would be entertaining in his own show.

Do you see the "fishing" success they had?

We hope you do.

Because we need to realize their record hauls were caught in the roughest conditions. They fished on rough proverbial seas, with many pirates in sight. They didn't catch enough to fry fish for the whole town many times over on bright sunny days, but rather did so in the blistering wind. They didn't catch the Bassmasters' record stringers on a smooth lake, but rather in conditions that would typically shut down a tournament.

The apostles made many disciples and did so in very uncertain times. They faced some of the most intense persecution in the history of Christianity and did so with extremely limited resources. It has been said that two constant characteristics of the early church were persecution and poverty.

The Apostle Paul wasn't one of the twelve, but he was responsible for bringing in many of these first-century disciples. Listen to him describe his fishing conditions in 2 Corinthians,

> *Five times I received from the Jews the forty lashes minus one. Three times I was beaten with rods, once I was pelted with stones, three times I was shipwrecked, I spent a night and a day in the open sea, I have been constantly on the move. I have been in danger from rivers, in danger from bandits, in danger from my fellow Jews, in danger from Gentiles; in danger in the city, in danger in the country, in danger at sea; and in danger from false believers. I have labored and toiled and have often gone without sleep; I have known hunger and thirst and have often gone without food; I have been cold and naked. Besides everything else, I face daily the pressure of my concern for all the churches (2 Corinthians 11:24-28).*

As fishers of men, we're not guaranteed nice fishing weather, but we're still called to make disciples.

# NOW

We wanted to title this devotion, "Keep Making Disciples," but unfortunately, in the USA, the statistics don't show we're making disciples. We should be. We need to start, and we can't wait for "better weather."

In uncertain times, we must make disciples.

And one bright spot in times of national distress is found in the fact that more disciples are made in rough times, rather than in times of ease.

Right now, Iran is the nation where the most disciples are being raised, and in Iran the church is underground. It's illegal to witness.

It's in these nations where it is dangerous to be a believer that we see more people being saved.

It's in these nations that the most sincere and faithful disciples are forged.

Though we're called to make disciples regardless of the uncertainty of the times, we should be excited to have the opportunity to be fishers of men in difficult days. We'll see an unbelievable harvest.

We must keep the mission given by Jesus before us, **"Therefore go and make disciples of all nations, baptizing them in the name of the Father and of the Son and of the Holy Spirit, and teaching them to obey everything I have commanded you" (Matthew 28:19-20, NIV).**

# INSTRUCTION FOR UNCERTAIN TIMES: MAKE DISCIPLES

# 39
## IN UNCERTAIN TIMES
# KNOW GOD

*Drawn from the truths presented in this book that have been gathered from the instruction and example of God's people facing great challenges.*

With each day's devotion, we've been compiling a list of what God does, and how God shows care to His people when they're in national or even personal distress. By no means is this list exhaustive, but you can be confident that you've been able to gain a picture of how God deals with His people when they're in uncertain times.

Many statements are made when the world's going crazy about what God must be doing, but often they're just clichéé statements devoid of critical consideration. Some of these statements are derived from Scripture but fail to extrapolate how God operates in difficult times.

Through this study, you've done this.

You've gained a truly biblical view of what God has done or is doing in those times.

This is important. When you're in uncertain times you can't let bad conditions shape your view of God and reality. Rather we must remember how God has revealed Himself in His Word. By knowing God and how He works, you can understand the times truthfully.

We're going to repost the truths we've gathered and we're now going to put them in order of how we believe you should reflect on them when difficulty comes. We also encourage you to conduct a study on the nature of God. Knowing His attributes will help you to understand what He's up to in trying times. You can check out our devotional book *Invincible* to learn more about His attributes.

Coupled with understanding the nature of God as revealed in the Scriptures, reflect on the following actions in this order when difficulty comes:

1. God Cares for His People

   *We need to lock this truth, of God and his dealings with us, in our minds and hearts. Often when there's silence, even in human relationships, we assume the worst about another party. Professionals warn that we should assume "positive intent." This may or may not be true in our relationships, but it is certainly true about God. Lay a foundation that no matter what happens, God cares about His people. He cares about you.*

2. God Has a Plan

   *Another foundational truth we need locked into our hearts is that no matter what happens, God has an ultimate plan. That plan isn't derailed by circumstances. Even if it doesn't make sense on our end, we need to trust God's plan is best.*

3. God Will Pull the Trigger

*One of the dangerous assumptions plaguing God's people concerning times of national distress is that God won't ever do something like pulling the trigger to discipline/punish us, or even allow it. He will. We must recognize that He will.*

4. God Will Bring His Word to Pass

*Fortunately, this means God will do the good He promised, but we also must know He will carry out the difficult things He promised. The bottom line is that whether the promise was good or bad, if it's in His Word, it will happen.*

5. God May Allow You to Suffer

*This is one of the bitterest pills to swallow, but God allows His people to suffer. We must remember that ultimately if we've trusted in Him as Savior then we'll one day receive perfect bodies with no more pain or suffering. We'll also enjoy eternal life, but, here and now, being His people doesn't make us exempt from suffering.*

6. God Warns

*This is another foundational truth about God that we need to sear into our hearts, because God will send warnings. If we don't realize difficulty and suffering can come, we're not going to be seeing clearly. The same is true about God's warnings. We must know God will warn so that we're looking for those warnings.*

7.  God Will Send Signs

    *This goes with the previous truth that God warns. His warnings come directly through prophets and the future-guiding of the Holy Spirit, but there also will be evident signs. We must keep our eyes open.*

8.  God Always Gives Hope

    *God wants us to know He desires to show love and mercy. Therefore, within any challenge, He has hope to give His people. There's always going to be a sunrise, no matter how dark the night.*

9.  God Could Be Punishing Sin

    *The first nine actions are foundational mindsets we must have. They help us not be controlled by circumstances and show us how to keep our eyes open. Beginning with this action, the remaining actions deal with our mindset and any actions we take within difficult circumstances. To help us know how to navigate a challenging time, we must realize God may be punishing us for sin.*

10. God Has Been Patient

*Because of what Scripture reveals about God, we can know that if God is punishing sin in our lives, or is punishing the sins of a nation, this isn't on a whim. God has already been patient if He is bringing punishment to pass.*

11. God Hears

*Once you're in distress and uncertainty, we should pray, and we should have confidence in praying because God hears.*

12. God Answers

*Furthermore, we should have confidence in praying because God answers. He wants us to ask Him and He wants to come through for us.*

13. God Will Send Reprieves

*Don't be surprised if in difficulty a break comes. Also, don't be surprised if the break is only temporary, for God often sends reprieves. But, with God, all calamity will end one day.*

14. God Will Relent but There May Be a Mess

*As mentioned, God will bring the difficulty in our lives or nation to an end in some way at some point, but there may still be a mess left. There may still be consequences we with which to deal.*

15. God Will Send Crazy Dreams

*This truth isn't as vital to know as the others, but we must know God speaks to His people with greater frequency and at greater volume in uncertain times. One of the major mediums He uses is dreams.*

If we know the attributes of God and how He responds to His people in tribulation, we'll be well on our way to being prepared to stand firm in uncertain times. Knowing about God is good, for throughout the ages and in the future, He doesn't change. As the prophet Malachi wrote: **"I the LORD do not change" (Malachi 3:6, NIV).**

# INSTRUCTION FOR UNCERTAIN TIMES: KNOW GOD

# 40

## IN UNCERTAIN TIMES
# BE PREPARED

*Drawn from the truths presented in this book that have been gathered from the instruction and example of God's people facing great challenges.*

This devotional book was birthed straight from the heart of Stand Firm Ministries, where we're encouraging and preparing believers to hold on to their faith in such times as these. Stand Firm came from the burden of the warning within Matthew 24:10 which warns that "many will turn away." At a minimum that means professed believers won't hear the words, "well done, my good and faithful servant" upon seeing the Lord. Now, that might not seem like such a big deal, but we guarantee you that, upon seeing the Lord, you will want to be found faithful.

At Stand Firm, we're driven by six *Stand Firm Scriptural Realities.*

1. Our faithfulness to God matters.

2. Our faithfulness to God is being challenged.

3. The Bible warns many will turn away.

4. You could be one that turns away.

5. Therefore, be a spiritual prepper and prepare to stand firm in these challenges.

6. Also, be a spiritual warrior, because standing firm isn't enough; we must march on to advance the Gospel.

Many have already walked away from the faith in the USA. Scriptural warnings and statistical evidence show that difficulty in life is the leading cause of this. Therefore, uncertain times are dangerous for our faith, but if we prepare before we face them, then we can stand firm.

There's no reason we can't or shouldn't be prepared for these difficult times because we have the beautifully written record of God's people in uncertain times; by looking at how they lived, or should have lived, we can better prepare ourselves. This has been the purpose of this 40-day study. We hope it's given you an awareness of how God's people have faced hardships and persevered in difficult times. During this daily journey, we've been compiling not just truths to know, but actions to live by. Not advice that's cliché, or man's wisdom, but tested truth from the Word, taken from the real challenges God's people have historically faced.

We've compiled two lists. The first you had in the previous devotion. It's a list of how God responds and cares for His people in times of difficulty. If we let those lay a foundational understanding of God, then we'll already be miles ahead when troubled times come. The lengthier list we've compiled deals with the actions we should take. The list is lengthy, but not exhaustive. Yet it provides sounds steps to keep us faithful in uncertain times. We've re-listed those here, not in the order they were presented in the devotional book, or how they unfolded in history, but we've thought through them and worked to place them in the order in which they should be acted upon. For most cases, the order isn't relative, but it certainly is for the ones at the top of the list. Since the list is so long, we provided only a little commentary when necessary on them, but they're self-explanatory. Our hope in this day's devotion is to remind you what you've read and for this to serve as a matrix you can continually utilize. As difficulty comes into your life, consider this a punch list to make sure you're doing what you can to endure and spiritually strive.

This day's devotion should also be a reminder of the absolute wonder of God's Word. It truly is sufficient. It truly does provide wisdom and help for our lives. Rita and I were overwhelmed in writing this final day, at that just how long this list had become, and how helpful it is for going through uncertain times. Please let this serve as a resource in uncertain times; be in awe of God's infinite wisdom; be challenged by the faith of those who've gone before us and commit to faithfully persevere in uncertain times.

## Before the Distress

1. Repent & Be Saved

*Ultimately, we must start our journey with Christ, by being saved. We talked about this on Day 36.*

207

2. Be Prepared

   *Don't wait until distress comes, but begin preparing ahead of time, for your faithfulness to God matters.*

3. Stay in Step with the Holy Spirit

   *We'll stand firm and strive if we're actively walking with God.*

4. Know God

   *Rest in the knowledge that He cares and has a plan. Understand that what He is doing is according to His nature and what He's done before.*

## In the Distress

5. Know God

   *This is listed twice on purpose. Beforehand we need to create a foundation of knowing how God will work in trying times, but also, when the trouble comes, we need to remind ourselves of how God cares and is working.*

6.  Check Your Ticket

    *Make sure you're where God wants you to be and adjust your life accordingly.*

7.  Repent

    *Ask God to search your heart and reveal sin, as He does, repent of all He reveals, and turn back to Him.*

8.  Keep the Vision and Make Disciples

    *Don't lose sight of your calling and mission.*

9.  Stick to Your Guns

10. Keep First Things First

11. Continue Spiritual Disciplines

12. Stay in the Word

13. Bet on God

14. Cry out to God

15. Pray

16. Boldly ask God

17. Trust God

18. Trust in God's Word

19. Be Brave

20. Be Obedient

21. Rise When Called

22. Be Willing to Burn

23. Be Bold

24. Boldly Ask Others

25. Keep Dreaming Dreams for God

26. Shine

27. Bust your Butt

Because we can look back at others who've stood firm and striven in uncertain times, we can prepare and follow their example. In warning about challenges that would come, Jesus told His disciples then and us today to prepare, **"You must also be ready" (Matthew 24:44, NIV).**

# INSTRUCTION FOR UNCERTAIN TIMES:
## BE PREPARED

# IF YOU FOUND THIS GUIDE HELPFUL,
# THEN YOU WILL LOVE <u>INVINCIBLE</u>.

ANOTHER STAND FIRM BOOK'S DEVOTIONAL FROM
JAKE MCCANDLESS AND RITA HALTER THOMAS.

GET YOUR COPY AT
WWW.STANDFIRMMINISTRIES.COM/BOOKS

# WOMEN!

## A STAND FIRM DEVOTIONAL
## JUST FOR YOU!

IT'S NOT ENOUGH TO JUST BE A SPIRITUAL PREPPER,
WE MUST ALSO BE SPIRITUAL WARRIORS.

*Available Now*

GET YOUR COPY AT
WWW.STANDFIRMMINISTRIES.COM/BOOKS

224

226

MORE RESOURCES CAN BE FOUND
AT
WWW.STANDFIRMMINISTRIES.COM

Made in the USA
Coppell, TX
12 October 2022

84529145R00134